BECOMING

A 365-Day Devotional for Students

KHIAN A. LAMEY

WESTBOW
PRESS®
A DIVISION OF THOMAS NELSON
& ZONDERVAN

WestBow Press books may be ordered through booksellers or by contacting:

WestBow Press
A Division of Thomas Nelson & Zondervan
1663 Liberty Drive
Bloomington, IN 47403
www.westbowpress.com
1 (866) 928-1240

Because of the dynamic nature of the Internet, any web addresses or links contained in this book may have changed since publication and may no longer be valid. The views expressed in this work are solely those of the author and do not necessarily reflect the views of the publisher, and the publisher hereby disclaims any responsibility for them.

Any people depicted in stock imagery provided by Getty Images are models, and such images are being used for illustrative purposes only. Certain stock imagery © Getty Images.

Scripture taken from the King James Version of the Bible.

Scripture taken from the Amplified Bible, Copyright © 1954, 1958, 1962, 1964, 1965, 1987 by The Lockman Foundation. Used with permission.

ISBN: 978-1-9736-4755-3 (sc)
ISBN: 978-1-9736-4757-7 (hc)
ISBN: 978-1-9736-4756-0 (e)

Library of Congress Control Number: 2018914414

Print information available on the last page.

WestBow Press rev. date: 11/27/2019

To The Glory of God

For Serena, Joshwray, Antonio, Josiah,
Terrique and Shenayah (Brithania)

The basis for your commitment
to having devotions

Psalm 5:3 (KJV)

> *My voice shalt thou hear in the morning, O LORD; in the*
> *morning will I direct my prayer unto thee, and will look up.*

Start each day by communicating with God.

DECLARATION: I commit to spending time with God at the start of my day.

DAY 1

AUGUST 1

Made In His Image

Genesis 1:27 (KJV)

> *So God created man in his own image, in the image of God created he him; male and female created he them.*

No matter how others describe you the fact remains; you are created in God's image. You have value. Yes, you are valuable. You see, God is the ruler of the world. He is sovereign. He is valuable. So, if you are made in His image it means that you are valuable.

God is perfect the way he is. He doesn't need longer hair or browner eyes. He is perfect. Our perfect Lord who knows all things made you in His image, so you are perfect.

PRAYER: Lord, thank You for creating me in Your image. I am valuable and perfect because I am made in Your image. You know all things and You made me just as I should be. Thank You in Jesus' name, amen.

DAY 2

AUGUST 2

The Gift of Salvation

John 3:16 (KJV)

> *For God so loved the world, that he gave his only begotten Son, that whosoever believeth in him should not perish, but have everlasting life.*

God loves me. Before I was born, before my parents thought of me, He sent His Son Jesus to die a brutal death for my sins. The reason Jesus died was that I, along with all people, can have everlasting life.

If you have never accepted Jesus as your savior please pray the following prayer:

> Lord, I have done things that are not right. I have sinned. I repent of my sins. Jesus, please come into my heart and save me. I believe you died on the cross for my sins; that you rose from the dead and is now seated at God's right hand. Please live in my heart forever. Fill me with the Holy Spirit. Thank You for saving me in Jesus' name, amen.

DECLARATION: I am saved. I have eternal life through Jesus. I am preparing myself to live successfully.

DAY 3

AUGUST 3

Serve the Lord

Joshua 24:15 (KJV)

> *And if it seem evil unto you to serve the LORD, choose you this day whom ye will serve; whether the gods which your fathers served that were on the other side of the flood, or the gods of the Amorites, in whose land ye dwell: but as for me and my house, we will serve the LORD.*

Each person must make a personal decision to serve God. Your parents' decision to serve God is not yours. While they introduce you to God and help you to develop a relationship with Him there will come a day when only you can decide that you are serving Him. Your friends should not decide whether you serve God or not. The choice is personal, it is yours. What will your decision be? Will you say yes to serving God, to a relationship with Him?

DECLARARTION: Today I choose to serve God. Today I choose Him as Lord over my life. Today I choose to accept Him as my personal Lord and Saviour.

DAY 4

AUGUST 4

The Blessing

Genesis 1: 28 (KJV)

And God blessed them, and God said unto them, Be fruitful, and multiply, and replenish the earth, and subdue it: and have dominion over the fish of the sea, and over the fowl of the air, and over every living thing that moveth upon the earth.

God blessed you before anyone could speak a negative word to you, over you or over you. It was an all-encompassing blessing. God is so gracious that He pre-empted man's curse with a blessing. Hallelujah! This means that no matter what people may call you, no matter what they may say that you cannot do, remember that God pronounced a blessing upon you when He made the earth, at the very beginning, and that blessing is still operating today. So be fruitful: produce good results and be productive, multiply: share your thoughts, ideas and skills with others to help them to be better people, replenish the earth: pray that the earth be filled with the glory of God, subdue the earth: control the forces of nature by being mindful of how you use the resources of the earth, and have dominion over the lesser creatures.

DECLARATION: I choose to live in God's blessings. I am fruitful. I produce good results and I am productive. I multiply. I share my thoughts, ideas and skills with others to help them to be better people. I replenish the earth. I pray that the earth will be filled with the glory of God. I subdue the earth. I control the forces of nature by being mindful of how I use the resources of the earth. I exercise dominion over the lesser creatures of the earth.

DAY 5

AUGUST 5

His Thoughts of Me

Jeremiah 29:11 (KJV)

> *For I know the thoughts that I think toward you, saith the LORD, thoughts of peace, and not of evil, to give you an expected end.*

God was thinking about you before He made the earth. How awesome! God has not stopped thinking about you. He still does. He has only good thoughts of you and He has ordained your end to be glorious.

DECLARATION: I am grateful for God's good thoughts towards me. Thank You God for thinking good things of me. Today I will think good thoughts about myself because that's what You think of me. I am beautiful. I am accomplished. I am intelligent.

AUGUST 6

Learning God's Laws

Psalm 119:33 (KJV)

> *Teach me, O LORD, the way of thy statutes; and I shall keep it unto the end.*

How awesome to know that we can ask God to be our teacher. Imagine the level of skill and patience that He takes to the job. His pedagogical skills are second to none. When God is your teacher you are guaranteed to pass the class. His statutes are His laws. They are many. Do not worry! Because of his extraordinary teaching skills, you will know and understand all of them. The only requirement is that you be a prepared student who is open and ready to learn. In preparation for classes pray 'Lord, teach me Your laws so that I can carry out my purpose to You and to humanity intelligently'.

DECLARATION: I prepare myself to be taught of the Lord. I am being taught by God. As God teaches me His statues I will obediently follow them.

DAY 7

AUGUST 7

Understanding

Psalm 119: 34 (KJV)

> *Give me understanding, and I shall keep thy law; yea, I shall observe it with my whole heart.*

Lord sometimes I do not understand what I am taught. However, beginning today I will ask for clarification when that happens. I begin this change in behavior by asking You to help me understand what You teach me so that I use that knowledge.

DECLARATION: God, by the Holy Spirit, will teach me. I understand and keep God's laws. When I do not understand what I am taught I will seek clarification from God and from my teachers.

DAY 8

AUGUST 8

Made to Live

Psalm 118:17 (KJV)

I shall not die, but live, and declare the works of the LORD.

Oftentimes we wonder why we were placed in the earth. Here is one reason – to declare, announce or assert God's work. That is, to tell others about what God has done and what He's doing. God has given you a lease on life so that you can tell everyone about His works. So, today tell someone about the works of God. It may be something astonishing, profound or quite simple. Sometimes we hear ourselves saying "I'm going to die" or "I want to die". Monitor your speech and instead of making those statements, declare that you will live. If you are not well, begin declaring that you will not die, but live and declare God's works! In Psalm 91 He promised to satisfy you with long life and show you His salvation. Therefore, speak life. Speak life over your body, your brain, your heart, your emotions and your dreams.

DECLARATION: I shall not die, but live, and declare the works of the LORD.

DAY 9

AUGUST 9

Keep Me From Wandering

Psalm 119:10 (KJV)

> *With my whole heart have I sought thee: O let me not wander
> from thy commandments.*

Sometimes we seek God partially, one foot in and one foot out. We are
reading the Bible but our mind is on the assignment that is due or the outfit
that we need to buy for the next function. However, we should seek God
wholeheartedly. So, let us pray.

> *Lord I am seeking You with all of my heart so please keep me
> in the way of Your commandment. You said in Your Word
> that if I seek You I will find You, if I seek You with all my
> heart. Take hold of my hands and quicken my steps.*

DECLARATION: As I seek the Lord with all of my heart He keeps me
from wandering from His commandments.

DAY 10

AUGUST 10

Increase!

Psalm 115:14 (KJV)

> *The L*ORD *shall increase you more and more, you and your children.*

God loves to give increase. He placed man in the earth and told him to multiply (increase). He sent His son Jesus who is the firstborn among many. He multiplies what we give to Him when He is returning things to us. His love for increase extends to your efforts. God will increase the results of your efforts. One day when you have children He will also increase the results of their efforts. In school you have to spend time reading or practicing so that you can understand the material. However, if you do not read, if you do nothing your increase or return will be nothing. Remember that zero multiplied by a thousand is zero. If you do not make an effort in school or in life the result will be zero. So, spend time doing your school work so that your efforts, when multiplied, will yield a large sum.

PRAYER: Lord, please help me to give much time to my studies so that my increase will be large.

DAY 11

AUGUST 11

Giving

Psalm 112:9 (AMP)

> *He has distributed freely [he has given to the poor and needy];*
> *his righteousness (uprightness and right standing with God)*
> *endures forever; his horn shall be exalted in honor.*

Are you a giver? Do you share what you have with others? Do you know a classmate who needs a pen? Do you know someone who needs a textbook that you used the previous semester? What do you do with such knowledge? Do offer to give your classmate a pen or the used textbook? Or, do you refuse to give your classmate one of the five pens that you have in your pencil case? When you give to those in need the Lord blesses you. Start making it a habit to give to those in need. In fact, look for opportunities to give. Remember that it is better to give than to receive.

DECLARATION: I understand the blessing of giving to those who have a need and I choose to give. I am a giver.

DAY 12

AUGUST 12

Praise!

Psalm 113:1 (KJV)

> *Praise ye the LORD. Praise, O ye servants of the LORD, praise the name of the LORD.*

To praise someone is to express compliment, approval or admiration of that person. When you praise God you are to express admiration of His character and His works. That is, you compliment Him approvingly. Can you think of statements that can be made in approval of God's character? Write down ten such statement. Now, how about His works? Write five of God's works that you admire. Read them aloud. Say them to Him. You just engaged in praise. There are many, many good things to say about God. Everything about God is good; you cannot exhaust all of them. Speak well of God each day. Sing new songs to Him. Praise ye the Lord.

DECLARATION: I will praise the Lord every day.

DAY 13

AUGUST 13

Why We Praise

Psalm 113:2-3 (KJV)

> *Blessed be the name of the LORD from this time forth and for evermore.*
>
> *From the rising of the sun unto the going down of the same the LORD's name is to be praised.*

The Lord's name is holy. It is sacred and every generation should recognize that. Being holy, God is deserving of your perpetual praise. Here the psalmist stated some of the reasons why Israel should praise God: the Lord is high above all nations, and His glory is above the heavens, He raises up the poor out of the dust, and lifts the needy out of the dunghill that He may set him with princes, He makes the barren woman to keep house, and to be a joyful mother of children.

Can you identify reasons to praise God from your nation's history, your family's history or your own experience?

DECLARATION: Blessed be the name of the LORD from this time and for evermore.

DAY 14

AUGUST 14

Your Inheritance

Genesis 25: 29 – 34 (AMP)

> *Jacob was boiling pottage (lentil stew) one day, when Esau came from the field and was faint [with hunger].*
>
> *And Esau said to Jacob, I beg of you, let me have some of that red lentil stew to eat, for I am faint and famished! That is why his name was called Edom [red].*
>
> *Jacob answered, Then sell me today your birthright (the rights of a firstborn).*
>
> *Esau said, See here, I am at the point of death; what good can this birthright do me?*
>
> *Jacob said, Swear to me today [that you are selling it to me]; and he swore to [Jacob] and sold him his birthright.*
>
> *Then Jacob gave Esau bread and stew of lentils, and he ate and drank and rose up and went his way. Thus Esau scorned his birthright as beneath his notice.*

Esau gave up all that he was entitled to receive when his father died for a bowl of stew. A bowl of stew! It is not wise to make permanent decisions in temporary situations. Neither is it a good thing to exploit people in their moment of weakness. When confronted with a decision that is likely to have long term impact, take some time to think about all the factors. Some factors are temporary, they will pass in a short time however; if acted upon, they are likely to have long-term effect. Be careful in your decision making.

DECLARATION: I will not make permanent decisions in temporary situations. I will not trade my inheritance in God for anything. I will not exploit others in their moment of weakness.

DAY 15

AUGUST 15

Protect the Dream

Genesis 37:18 (KJV)

> *And when they saw him afar off, even before he came near*
> *unto them, they conspired against him to slay him.*

Do you have a dream that is so big that you sometimes wonder if it will ever become reality? Have you thought about implementing a system, a programme or creating a product or organization that will make things easier for your family, your community, your country, the world? Did you ever share that dream with someone who tried to dissuade you from dreaming or working towards making the dream come true? If yes, do not be discouraged by negative feedback. Instead, ask God to direct you to the persons who will support and nurture your dreams.

DECLARATION: I will work towards accomplishing my dreams. I refuse to kill the dreams of another person. Instead I will assist others to live their dreams.

DAY 16

AUGUST 16

Genesis 39:3 (KJV)

And his master saw that the LORD was with him, and that the LORD made all that he did to prosper in his hand.

It is possible for people to look at you and see that God is in you. It is also possible for people to look at you and see that He is with you. God's presence was all-encompassing in Joseph's life. This was evident as his master, who was not a Christian, recognized that God was with him. You can have God with you by asking Him to remain with you and then creating an environment for Him to be with you at all times. You create that environment by reading the Bible, praying, fasting, praising, worshipping and listening to recorded sermons.

DECLARATION: I choose to live my life so that all those who I come in contact with, especially those in authority, will see that God is with me.

DAY 17

AUGUST 17

Putting Myself Together Well

Genesis 41:14 (KJV)

> *Then Pharaoh sent and called Joseph, and they brought him hastily out of the dungeon: and he shaved himself, and changed his raiment, and came in unto Pharaoh.*

People judge you by different things – what you say, what you do and what you wear. However, no matter what the occasion, one basis rule apply to your dressing : be careful to always appear neat and clean. Also, it is important to dress according to where you are going, according to the occasion. As a student it is very likely that you have a prescribed uniform; ensure that it is well-fitted, clean and neatly ironed. If you do not wear a uniform to school ensure that your attire is clean and modest. Finally, it is most important to remember that when you are among people their nostrils will not go on vacation; it will still continue to work, therefore; pay keen attention to your personal hygiene.

DECLARATION: I will always dress appropriately according to my audience. My uniform must always be neat and well-fitted. I will also pay close attention to my personal hygiene.

DAY 18

AUGUST 18

Creation

Genesis 1:1 (KJV)

In the beginning God created the heaven and the earth.

In the beginning God! God was at the beginning. Incredible as it may sound, He was at the beginning of time. In fact, He called time into existence. He gave time existence. At the very beginning of time as we know it, God created the heaven and the earth. There is no theory that can explain the creation of heaven and earth. The Bible provides the report – in the beginning God created the heaven and the earth. The Holy Spirit was there when it happened and He guided the writing of the Bible. Theorists were not there when the earth was being created. Will you believe the firsthand account of the Holy Spirit or the speculations of theorists?

DECLARATION: God is the creator of heaven and earth and I acknowledge and accept His authority.

DAY 19

AUGUST 19

The Purpose of Proverbs

Proverbs 1:1 (AMP)

> *The proverbs (truths obscurely expressed, maxims, and parables) of Solomon son of David, king of Israel:*
>
> *That people may know skillful and godly wisdom and instruction, discern and comprehend the words of understanding and insight*

If you read to verse 6 of Proverbs chapter 1 you will be able to identify the fifteen purposes of the proverbs of King Solomon. If you read, study and apply the proverbs you will see the manifestation of all fifteen purposes in your life. Take the challenge today.

PRAYER: Lord, please give me grace to diligently read the book of Proverbs and practice the principles so that I will see the purposes of the proverbs in in my life. I pray this in Jesus' name, amen.

AUGUST 20

The Purpose of Proverbs II

Proverbs 1:3-6 (KJV)

> *To know wisdom and instruction; to perceive the words of understanding;*
>
> *To receive the instruction of wisdom, justice, and judgment, and equity;*
>
> *To give subtilty to the simple, to the young man knowledge and discretion.*
>
> *A wise man will hear, and will increase learning; and a man of understanding shall attain unto wise counsels:*
>
> *To understand a proverb, and the interpretation; the words of the wise, and their dark sayings.*

It is amazing that God would give us such insightful information. He has given us all things that pertain to life and godliness: (2 Peter 1:3). Today we take time to pray based on other purposes of the proverbs.

PRAYER: O that I may know wisdom and instruction; that I will perceive the words of understanding. Lord, I receive wisdom, justice, judgment and equity. By knowledge of the proverbs I have prudence and wisdom;

knowledge and discretion. I hear the proverbs, I read them, I meditate on them and I increase learning and succeed in attaining wise counsels. I thank You Lord that I understand parables, the clever saying and riddles of the wise.

DAY 21

AUGUST 21

He Does Not Forget What He Says

Genesis 15:13-14 (KJV)

> *And he said unto Abram, Know of a surety that thy seed shall be a stranger in a land that is not theirs, and shall serve them; and they shall afflict them four hundred years;*

> *And also that nation, whom they shall serve, will I judge: and afterward shall they come out with great substance.*

Exodus 1:13-14 (KJV)

> *And the Egyptians made the children of Israel to serve with rigour:*

> *And they made their lives bitter with hard bondage, in morter, and in brick, and in all manner of service in the field: all their service, wherein they made them serve, was with rigour.*

Exodus 12:31-36, 40 (AMP)

> *[Pharaoh] called for Moses and Aaron by night, and said, Rise up, get out from among my people, both you and the Israelites; and go, serve the Lord, as you said.*

Also take your flocks and your herds, as you have said, and be gone! And [ask your God to] bless me also.

The Egyptians were urgent with the people to depart, that they might send them out of the land in haste; for they said, We are all dead men.

The people took their dough before it was leavened, their kneading bowls being bound up in their clothes on their shoulders.

The Israelites did according to the word of Moses; and they [urgently] asked of the Egyptians jewels of silver and of gold, and clothing.

The Lord gave the people favor in the sight of the Egyptians, so that they gave them what they asked. And they stripped the Egyptians [of those things].

Now the time the Israelites dwelt in Egypt was 430 years.

PRAYER: Lord please help me to believe the Words You speak over my life, no matter how long they take to be fulfilled. I am grateful that You exalted your Words above Your name and You watch over Your words to perform them.

DAY 22

AUGUST 22

The Blessing of a Priest

Numbers 6: 22-27 (AMP)

And the Lord said to Moses,

> *Say to Aaron and his sons, This is the way you shall bless the Israelites.*
>
> *Say to them,*
>
> *The Lord bless you and watch, guard, and keep you;*
>
> *The Lord make His face to shine upon and enlighten you and be gracious (kind, merciful, and giving favor) to you;*
>
> *The Lord lift up His [approving] countenance upon you and give you peace (tranquility of heart and life continually).*
>
> *And they shall put My name upon the Israelites, and I will bless them.*

God authored the blessing that Aaron, the high priest, was to speak over the children of Israel. When those words were spoken, God blessed them. It is important that you submit to your father, the priest of your home. It is also important that you submit to the spiritual authority at your church.

25

These persons are empowered to bless you. Ask your pastor and father to bless you today.

CONFESSION: The Lord thinks of everything concerning His people, even the minutest detail is not overlooked. I trust in Him.

DAY 23

AUGUST 23

The Glory of God

Numbers 14:21 (KJV)

> *But as truly as I live, all the earth shall be filled with the glory of the LORD.*

The glory of God is His manifested presence, the beauty of His spirit. There are innumerable ways in which we see God's beauty – in His faithfulness, His kindness, His providence, His holiness, His greatness. God said that as truly as He lives the earth will be filled with His glory. God is sovereign. We know that no matter what happens He will not die therefore; the earth will always be filled with His glory. So, we can awake each day in expectation of seeing the glory of God in the earth.

DECLARATION: I believe in God who will never die. I will see God's glory in the earth. The earth is filled with the glory of God. My hope will always be in God.

DAY 24

AUGUST 24

God Cannot Lie

Numbers 23:19 (KJV)

> *God is not a man, that he should lie; neither the son of man,*
> *that he should repent: hath he said, and shall he not do it? or*
> *hath he spoken, and shall he not make it good?*

So many times those who we trust, those who we look up to, lie to us. Sometimes, when caught in a bind little white lies are told to escape the consequences. Lying breaches trust and causes deep pain. How awesome it is to know that God cannot lie. How assuring to know that God will never lie! It is reassuring to know that we can stand on God's promises and He will never have to apologize because He cannot fulfill a promise He has made. This wonderful assurance settles the confidence of all who trust in God. This knowledge will also help others to trust Him.

CONFESSION: Because of God's integrity I trust Him completely.

DAY 25

AUGUST 25

He Is Jealous of Me

Deuteronomy 4:24 (KJV)

For the LORD thy God is a consuming fire, even a jealous God.

A consuming fire. That is a fire that totally consumes anything that is in its path. Our loving Father God is a consuming fire. He does not want us to be given to idolatry. God does not want us to put anything or anyone above Him. He wants to be first in our lives. God is jealous of you. He wants you to be holy and will totally destroy anything in our lives that is unholy. As Moses did with the children of Israel, God warns us before He destroys. For all that God has done for us the least we can do is to serve Him in truth and holiness. Place Him first. Do not allow anything or anyone to complete for pride of place in your life. Reserve that place for God.

DECLARATION: I will place God first in my life. I will serve Him with all my heart knowing that He is very jealous of me.

AUGUST 26

Life Lessons

Deuteronomy 6: 4-5 (KJV)

But you who clung fast to the Lord your God are alive, every one of you, this day.

Behold, I have taught you statutes and ordinances as the Lord my God commanded me, that you should do them in the land which you are entering to possess.

People who hold on tenaciously to God live. No matter what is happening to them or around them, God will keep and protect them. They have confidence in an integrous God. You are being taught God's laws at Sunday School, Sabbath School, Youth Meeting, church, home and school. These lessons will keep you as you grow older and enter into different careers, professions and trades. You are to practice them everywhere you go. No matter what situation you face today or in the future, confidently cling to God. Do not forsake then. In fact, you should apply them every day wherever life takes you.

DECLARATION: By God's grace I will keep His laws all the days of my life. I will hold fast to them and I shall live.

DAY 27

AUGUST 27

He Is Faithful

Deuteronomy 7:9 (KJV)

> *Know therefore that the LORD thy God, he is God, the faithful*
> *God, which keepeth covenant and mercy with them that love*
> *him and keep his commandments to a thousand generations;*

God's character is impeccable. He is a covenant keeping God. He faithfully keeps His covenants to a thousand generations! Can you imagine to how many of your family members He will be faithful to? There are many covenants in the Bible that you can part-take of simply because you accepted the gift of salvation and is now an heir to the promises God made to Abraham. Ask the Holy Spirit to guide you to covenants and plead them before God. You will be surprised at what begins to happen in your life.

PRAYER: Lord, I praise You for who You are, in Jesus' name. Amen.

DAY 28

AUGUST 28

Full Praise

Deuteronomy 8:10 (KJV)

> *When thou hast eaten and art full, then thou shalt bless the*
> *LORD thy God for the good land which he hath given thee.*

Always bless God in times of plenty. When things are going well, when there is an abundance people usually rely on themselves and not acknowledge the goodness of God. However, it is important to bless God in these times. When you pass the test, when you are promoted to a new class, when you win the election to a position in student government, is an apt time to bless God for the good things He has given you.

DECLARATION: I will bless God in times of plenty.

AUGUST 29

Investing For Tomorrow

Deuteronomy 8:18 (KJV)

> *But thou shalt remember the Lord thy God: for it is he that giveth thee power to get wealth, that he may establish his covenant which he sware unto thy fathers, as it is this day.*

Pause. Imagine that you couldn't breathe. Imagine that you had no backbone. Imagine that you had no brain. Think. God gave you breath. He gave you a backbone. He gave you a brain. These things, and others, enable you to attend school and learn so that you can be an effective member of society later. These are your years of preparing for the future. What you invest now will determine the dividend payable later. Therefore, it is important to use your brain and other faculties to ensure that you lay the foundation for a great adult life.

DECLARATION: These are my preparation years. I am laying the foundation for wealth creation. I will invest wisely so that I will be paid a sizable dividend later.

DAY 30

AUGUST 30

Deuteronomy 6:20 (KJV)

> *And when thy son asketh thee in time to come, saying, What mean the testimonies, and the statutes, and the judgments, which the LORD our God hath commanded you?*

Do you understand why your parents worship God? Do you understand why a tenth of their income is given to God every month? Do you understand why Mommy cries in worship? Do you understand what happens to Daddy when the Holy Ghost comes upon Him? Do you understand why Mommy goes to visit the old lady who has no family? Do you understand why Mommy tells the same stories of how God helped her? If not, ask.

DECLARATION: I will ask my parents the meaning of the things of God. Their answer will help me to develop a love and relationship with God. My questioning will initiate conversation which will result in a closer relationship between us.

DAY 31

AUGUST 31

Doing My Part

Deuteronomy 28:1-2 (KJV)

> *And it shall come to pass, if thou shalt hearken diligently unto the voice of the LORD thy God, to observe and to do all his commandments which I command thee this day, that the LORD thy God will set thee on high above all nations of the earth:*

> *And all these blessings shall come on thee, and overtake thee, if thou shalt hearken unto the voice of the LORD thy God.*

The Lord has promised numerous blessings if you listen to and do His commandments. Read verses 3 – 14. You will notice that these blessings are conditional. They are given if you are obedient. They are blessings for obedience. These blessings will come upon you – they will be visible in your life – and they will go before you. That is, before you reach a place, even while on your way, the blessing will show up there. To do what God requires, you have to know what He requires. Therefore, you will have to study and meditate upon His Word – the Bible. Set your alarm to get up for personal Bible study.

CONFESSION: I will read God's Word. I will listen to God's Word. I will do all the things that His Word tells me to do. I choose to do all that God's Word tells me to do.

DAY 32

SEPTEMBER 1

Courage

Joshua 1:7 (KJV)

> *Only be thou strong and very courageous, that thou mayest observe to do according to all the law, which Moses my servant commanded thee: turn not from it to the right hand or to the left, that thou mayest prosper withersoever thou goest.*

God commanded Joshua to be strong and very courageous. Strength and courage are important virtues. They are especially important for leaders to have. Strength and courage can be learnt. Your parents, teachers and pastors have taught you and are teaching you some invaluable lessons about how to develop these character traits. Do not walk away from them. Do not ignore them. Consciously decide to follow them and you will be richly rewarded.

DECLARATION: I will observe to do all the things God require of me. All the things that God require of me are in the Bible. My parents, teachers and pastors have taught and are teaching them to me.

DAY 33

SEPTEMBER 2

God Is With Me!

Joshua 1:9 (KJV)

Have not I commanded thee? Be strong and of a good courage;
be not afraid, neither be thou dismayed: for the Lord *thy*
God is with thee whithersoever thou goest.

God commanded Joshua to be strong, courageous, bold, secure, confidence, calm and composed because wherever he went He (God) would be there with him. Today God is with you in the form of the Holy Ghost therefore, you have the same assurance as Joshua did. So develop strength, courage and boldness. Exercise calmness. Be strong, courageous, bold, secure, confident, calm and composed because God is with you. Knowing that God is with you provides additional confidence to exhibit these character traits in your daily life.

DECLARATION: I am strong, courageous, bold, secure, confident, calm and composed because God will be with me wherever I go.

DAY 34

SEPTEMBER 3

No Impossibility

Joshua 10:12-14 (KJV)

> *Then spake Joshua to the LORD in the day when the LORD delivered up the Amorites before the children of Israel, and he said in the sight of Israel, Sun, stand thou still upon Gibeon; and thou, Moon, in the valley of Ajalon.*
>
> *And the sun stood still, and the moon stayed, until the people had avenged themselves upon their enemies.*

God is very fascinating. He is also all-powerful. He creates and controls time. When the children of Israel were in battle with the Amorites, Joshua commanded and God caused time to stand still. This means that the earth stop revolving around the sun! God listened to His servant and caused the elements to align with his words. This was done to enable the children of Israel to win a battle! Imagine what He will do for you.

DECLARATION: God can do the things that I think are impossible. I will not try to limit His ability in my mind or with my words. I will ask Him to do the things that seem impossible to me.

DAY 35

SEPTEMBER 4

Know The Word

Joshua 18:3 (KJV)

> *And Joshua said unto the children of Israel, How long are ye slack to go to possess the land, which the LORD God of your fathers hath given you?*

When the children of Israel entered Canaan they were given various lands to possess. However, despite being given the land some had not taken the initiative to possess it. Sometimes God give us things – gifts, talents and abilities – that we do not use. Doing this is the same as some tribes of the children of Israel did. It is important that you possess, use and exploit the gifts, talents and abilities that God has given you. The Bible is God's Word to you. It contains all His promises and instructions. Do you know all that are in it? Before you can possess or claim God's promises you must know them. Therefore begin OPERATION BIBLE STUDY to get to know them.

DECLARATION: I will study the Bible to know God's promises and instructions to me. As I become aware of them I will own them.

DAY 36

SEPTEMBER 5

Serve God Honestly

Joshua 24: 22-23 (KJV)

> *And Joshua said unto the people, Ye are witnesses against yourselves that ye have chosen you the LORD, to serve him. And they said, We are witnesses.*

> *Now therefore put away, said he, the strange gods which are among you, and incline your heart unto the LORD God of Israel.*

Sometimes people choose to serve God but retain things like the latest dancehall, hip hop or soca song on their phone. Or, they continue to attend the trendy clubs to have a good time. They make time to watch their favourite artiste or go to concerts that the artiste is performing at but refuse to make time to pray. In doing so, those things are made into idols. Persons who elevate things above God commit idolatry. When you decide to serve God you should give up the things that do not glorify Him. God is jealous. He wants all of you. You have to give your heart completely to Him. What do you need to put away to truly serve God?

PRAYER: Lord, please forgive me for serving other gods. From today I will serve only You.

DAY 37

SEPTEMBER 6

Learn From the Elders

Judges 2:10 (KJV)

> *And also all that generation were gathered unto their fathers:*
> *and there arose another generation after them, which knew*
> *not the LORD, nor yet the works which he had done for Israel.*

When Joshua and his peers died the younger persons who were growing into adulthood did not know God. They did not know what He had done for their nation. One of two things happened: they were not taught or they did not care to learn. It is important that you learn who God is and what He has done from persons who are older than you are, especially persons in your family and in the body of Christ. They will not be around forever. Their stories will educated and inform you. They will make sure that when you become an adult you know God and are able to avoid doing things that are against His will. Also, one day you will have children and will need to teach them who God is and what He has done. If you do not know, you will not be able to teach them.

DECLARATION: I will learn about God and what He has done from persons who are older than I am.

DAY 38

SEPTEMBER 7

Mentorship

Ruth 1:16 (KJV)

> *And Ruth said, Intreat me not to leave thee, or to return from following after thee: for whither thou goest, I will go; and where thou lodgest, I will lodge: thy people shall be my people, and thy God my God:*

Ruth was Naomi's daughter-in-law. Her husband, Naomi's son, was dead. Naomi's husband was also dead. As a result of this Naomi, who was experiencing extreme poverty, decided to go back to her original country. Ruth decided to accompany her but along the way Naomi tried to dissuade her. This caused Ruth to beg her not to do so. She also vowed to go with Naomi and take her nationality. Because Ruth was persistent Naomi allowed her to accompany her home and later advised her on a relationship that led to marriage and the end of their poverty. Mentors have travelled the road on which you about to start a journey. They can provide invaluable advice and guidance.

DECLARATION: I will look for and pursue great mentors.

DAY 39

SEPTEMBER 8

Pay The Vow

Psalm 76:11 (KJV)

Vow, and pay unto the LORD your God: let all that be round about him bring presents unto him that ought to be feared.

Have you ever prayed a prayer that essentially said 'God if you do 'x' I will do 'y'? If you have, you made a vow to God. Oftentimes once God does what we ask Him to, we quickly forget about our vow – what we pledged to do. This is very unbecoming. It is also very dishonest. There is no obligation to make a vow to God so if you do, be responsible and keep that vow. Pay the vow. Be honest in your dealings with God. Doing so will help you to be honest in your dealings with men.

DECLARATION: If I make I vow to God I will honour Him by paying it.

SEPTEMBER 9

Pursuit

1 Samuel 1:11; 27-28 (KJV)

> *And she vowed a vow, and said, O LORD of hosts, if thou wilt indeed look on the affliction of thine handmaid, and remember me, and not forget thine handmaid, but wilt give unto thine handmaid a man child, then I will give him unto the LORD all the days of his life, and there shall no razor come upon his head.*
>
> *For this child I prayed; and the LORD hath given me my petition which I asked of him:*
>
> *Therefore also I have lent him to the LORD; as long as he liveth he shall be lent to the LORD. And he worshipped the LORD there.*

Hannah wanted a baby but she could not have one. She prayed to God and promised that if He gave her a boy baby she would give him back to God and his hair would not be trimmed. The promise she made to God was her vow. When the baby was born Hannah kept her promise by taking him to the temple to serve there. She paid her vow.

Do you need something from God desperately? Hannah's prayer is a model: pray and make a vow. When God answers be sure to do what you promised to do.

DECLARATION: Like Hannah, I will pay my vows to God.

DAY 41

SEPTEMBER 10

Better Not To Vow

Ecclesiastes 5:4-5 (KJV)

> *When thou vowest a vow unto God, defer not to pay it; for he hath no pleasure in fools: pay that which thou hast vowed.*
>
> *Better is it that thou shouldest not vow, than that thou shouldest vow and not pay.*

People sometimes make vows lightly. It is made in one breath and forgotten in the other. However, Solomon warns that if you make a vow to God you must pay it. God is sovereign. He outranks all men therefore you must honour any promise made to him. In fact, Solomon implies that if you dishonor your vow to God you are a fool. A fool lacks judgment; he is a stupid person. Is that a description that you want to be spoken of you? If you do not intend to keep a vow, do not make it. It is better not to make a vow to God than to make one and not fulfill it.

PRAYER: Lord, please help me to develop the discipline and integrity to pay my vows to you.

DAY 42

SEPTEMBER 12

Obey Your Parents

1 Samuel 3:4-5 (KJV)

That the LORD called Samuel: and he answered, Here am I.

And he ran unto Eli, and said, Here am I; for thou calledst me. And he said, I called not; lie down again. And he went and lay down

Do you delay in responding when your parent or an adult calls? It is always tempting to delay a response, especially if the book you're reading or movie you are watching is at an interesting point. Sometime you just don't want to be disturbed and pretend not to hear the call. However, no matter what you are doing, you should promptly respond to the call of your parent or an adult. Samuel's prompt response to what he believed to be Eli's call demonstrates respect and obedience. Likewise, when you respond promptly to your parents you are showing them respect and obedience. Respect and obedience are character traits that will look good in and on you.

CONFESSION: I will promptly respond when my parents' call. I will promptly respond when an adult calls. My prompt response is obedience.

DAY 43

SEPTEMBER 11

Speak Lord

1 Samuel 3:7-10 (KJV)

> *Now Samuel did not yet know the LORD, neither was the word of the LORD yet revealed unto him.*
>
> *And the LORD called Samuel again the third time. And he arose and went to Eli, and said, Here am I; for thou didst call me. And Eli perceived that the LORD had called the child.*
>
> *Therefore Eli said unto Samuel, Go, lie down: and it shall be, if he call thee, that thou shalt say, Speak, LORD; for thy servant heareth. So Samuel went and lay down in his place.*
>
> *And the LORD came, and stood, and called as at other times, Samuel, Samuel. Then Samuel answered, Speak; for thy servant heareth.*

When Samuel first heard God he did not recognize the voice. He had never heard God's voice before and so when he heard it he thought that Eli the priest had called him. However Eli realized that it was God talking to Samuel so he told him how to respond. A very popular question is 'how do I know God's voice? How do I distinguish His voice from my thoughts?' We have to learn to hear God's voice. Persons who are more mature in the faith will be able to help you to discern God's voice, just like Eli helped Samuel. Notice that after consulting with Eli, when God called Samuel again he promptly responded as Eli told him to. God still speaks in an audible voice. Have you ever heard Him? Do you know His voice?

PRAYER: Lord, I will listen for Your voice. Please help me to identify it. Father let my ears be always sensitive to Your voice. I will promptly respond to You Father.

DAY 44

SEPTEMBER 13

Adopting Good Example

1 Samuel 8:1, 3 (KJV)

> *And it came to pass, when Samuel was old, that he made his sons judges over Israel.*
>
> *And his sons walked not in his ways, but turned aside after lucre, and took bribes, and perverted judgment.*

Samuel was a judge in Israel. Historically parents groomed their children to join their profession. Sometimes children are even groomed to take over businesses upon the retirement of parents. In the same way, when Samuel became old he made his sons judges but they did not model his exemplary behavior. Instead they departed from his example and sought personal and selfish gain, took bribes and perverted justice. They did not reap the benefits that they could if they had adopted their father's good example and walk before the Lord in truth and righteousness. Your parents or someone in your family is providing an excellent spiritual example for you. Choose to follow that example all the days of your life.

PRAYER: Lord, please give me grace to follow the good examples that adults are setting for me, in Jesus' name. Amen.

DAY 45

SEPTEMBER 14

Tough Love

Proverbs 3:11-12 (AMP)

> *My son, do not despise or shrink from the chastening of the Lord [His correction by punishment or by subjection to suffering or trial]; neither be weary of or impatient about or loathe or abhor His reproof,*
>
> *For whom the Lord loves He corrects, even as a father corrects the son in whom he delights.*

Sometimes we think of God as a friend and not as a parent who corrects us when we do wrong. Every loving parent corrects a child who has done wrong. Correction is demonstration of love for the child. When God corrects us He is showing His love for us. He is helping to groom us into exemplary human beings. God corrects those who He loves. Imagine if your parents did not tell you the difference between wrong and right. What if Mommy says "O baby, it's ok to steal Daddy's money". Where are you likely to end up in a few years?

PRAYER: Lord, I thank You for correcting me and I will not shrink from it. I will not loathe Your reproof in Jesus' name, amen.

DAY 46

SEPTEMBER 15

Be an Example

1 Timothy 4:12 (KJV)

> *Let no man despise thy youth; but be thou an example of the believers, in word, in conversation, in charity, in spirit, in faith, in purity.*

Even though Timothy was young Paul encouraged him to be an example to the believers. You too, though young, are to be an example to the believers. Be an example by –

- believing the Word of God, nothing else.
- ensuring that your conversations are good. Are the conversations you have with your school friends the same as you have with your church friends.
- showing God's love to everyone, not a select few.
- having a good attitude in doing your tasks and in communicating with others.
- being faithful and pure.
- being respectful and honest.

PRAYER: Lord, please give me grace to be an example to other believers.

DAY 47

SEPTEMBER 16

Face Fear Squarely

1 Samuel 17:26 (KJV)

> *And David spake to the men that stood by him, saying, What shall be done to the man that killeth this Philistine, and taketh away the reproach from Israel? for who is this uncircumcised Philistine, that he should defy the armies of the living God?*

Goliath was a huge man. He was a giant. He was taller and bigger than the soldiers in the army of Israel. He challenged them and they were afraid. They were so fearful of him that when they saw him they ran away. However, David identified him as an enemy who had no right to stand against the army of Israel.

Sometimes students hear that a subject is hard and they run away before they even attempt it. Even before a student reaches grade two they are known to say say 'Maths is hard, I can't do it.' Do not run away in fear. Instead, identify the things that are challenging to you. Like David, choose to face anything that is telling you that you can't. You are God's child. Like the army of Israel was His army, you are His. He made you to be victorious. When you face your fears you'll conquer them.

DECLARATION: I am a child of God. I will face and overcome all my fears by the grace of God.

DAY 48

SEPTEMBER 17

Prepare

1 Samuel 17:40 (KJV)

> *And he took his staff in his hand, and chose him five smooth stones out of the brook, and put them in a shepherd's bag which he had, even in a scrip; and his sling was in his hand: and he drew near to the Philistine.*

David knew that he was going to fight Goliath and he made preparation. The first thing he did was to take up his staff – a stick that provided support. The second thing he did was to choose five stones from the stream. The word choose suggest that he did not randomly take up stones but was selective. The third thing that David did was to put the stones in his bag. The fourth thing he did was to take his slingshot in his hand. Having his readied himself, he faced Goliath.

Preparation is a key ingredient for success. Whether you want to overcome a limitation or achieve a goal, you must prepare. Prepare. Prepare. Prepare. Your preparation cannot be without consideration, it should be systematic. You must prepare to succeed. To succeed as a student you should make a study timetable and follow it, read ahead of your teacher, participate in class activities, ask questions and do homework. Preparation also includes being honest about the areas or subjects in which you are having difficulty. You should tell your parents and teachers so that arrangements can be made for you to get the necessary help to enable you to succeed.

DECLARATION: I will prepare for my success.

DAY 49

SEPTEMBER 18

Faithful Friends

Exodus 17:11-13 (KJV)

> *And it came to pass, when Moses held up his hand, that Israel prevailed: and when he let down his hand, Amalek prevailed.*
>
> *But Moses hands were heavy; and they took a stone, and put it under him, and he sat thereon; and Aaron and Hur stayed up his hands, the one on the one side, and the other on the other side; and his hands were steady until the going down of the sun.*
>
> *And Joshua discomfited Amalek and his people with the edge of the sword.*

The children of Israel were in battle. They were fighting Amalek. Before the actual fighting began Moses told Joshua to choose men to go into battle and he would stand on the top of the hill with the rod of God in his hand. Joshua went to battle and Moses stood on top of the hill. Israel won when Moses held up his hand but they started losing whenever his hand fell. Recognizing what was happening two faithful men – Aaron and Hur - went to assist. They made Moses sit and each of them held up one of his hands, causing the children of Israel to win the battle. Who are the persons who will be there for you in hard times? Who are the persons who will be there for you when your strength is waning? Who are the persons who will hold up your hands? Will you be an Aaron or Hur for a friend or leader?

PRAYER: Lord, make me a faithful friend and colleague. Father, please give me faithful friends and colleagues in Jesus' name, amen.

DAY 50

SEPTEMBER 19

Strengthen Your Friends

1 Samuel 23:16 (KJV)

And Jonathan Saul's son arose, and went to David into the wood, and strengthened his hand in God.

Jonathan was David's friend. His father wanted to kill David because he was jealous of him. As a result, to avoid being killed, David went to live in the woods. Despite what his father was doing, Johnathan continued being David's friend and even went to visit him in the woods. By doing so he risked the ire of his father but their friendship was of such value to him. It is important to have friends who will be there for you in difficult times. It is important to be committed to your friends. This commitment should be demonstrated by your support for your friends, especially in difficult times.

CONFESSION: I will support my friends in their time of need.

DAY 51

SEPTEMBER 20

Encourage Yourself

1 Samuel 30:6 (KJV)

> *And David was greatly distressed; for the people spake of stoning him, because the soul of all the people was grieved, every man for his sons and for his daughters: but David encouraged himself in the LORD his God.*

Life is funny. You may have a cheering squad today and tomorrow you are the only one present at your recital. You may not have anyone to cheer you on or support your dreams but determine to be your own cheerleader and cheerleading team. This may be distressing but there is no shame in it. If you find yourself in this situation, it does not mean that you are not loved or that you are worse off than someone else. Begin to encourage yourself in the Lord today.

DECLARATION: I will encourage myself in the Lord.

DAY 52

SEPTEMBER 21

Grace to Lead

1Kings 3:5 (KJV)

In Gibeon the LORD appeared to Solomon in a dream by night: and God said, Ask what I shall give thee.

Solomon was young when he became the king of Israel. He did not think that he could lead the nation successfully, so he asked God for understanding. God gave him understanding and today he is referred to as the wisest man who ever lived. Leadership can be daunting, especially when you are young and inexperienced. You may have chosen or were chosen to lead a group at church or at school and now you are wondering how you are going to do it successfully. Despite the uncertainty in your own ability to lead, this is no reason for you to shy away from the opportunity to develop new skills. As Solomon did, you too can ask God for understanding and wisdom to excel in your new position or office.

PRAYER: Lord, according to Your word, please give me wisdom that I may excel in leadership, that I may discern truth and rightly perform the functions of my office for Your glory.

SEPTEMBER 23

Wisdom: The Principal Thing

Proverbs 4:7 (AMP)

> *The beginning of Wisdom is: get Wisdom (skillful and godly Wisdom)! [For skillful and godly Wisdom is the principal thing.] And with all you have gotten, get understanding (discernment, comprehension, and interpretation).*

Having good judgment, intelligence, insight, perception and knowledge is very important. Therefore get the Godly kind. Wisdom is the principal thing. It is the main or the most important thing when things are arranged in order of importance. Because it is the principal thing, you cannot afford to neglect it. Proverbs 1: 20-24 tells about wisdom crying in the streets and the simple rejecting her counsel. You can get wisdom by asking God for it. Wisdom will change your life; it will take you to places that you have never dreamed of. When you are asking God for wisdom, ask Him for understanding also. Understanding is the perfect complement to wisdom.

DECLARATION: I have the wisdom of God to skillfully accomplish my tasks. Leaders of nations will call me to solve problems. I have understanding to do all that is required of me in Jesus' name. Amen.

DAY 54

SEPTEMBER 22

Ask for Wisdom

James 1:5 (KJV)

> *If any of you lack wisdom, let him ask of God, that giveth to all men liberally, and upbraideth not; and it shall be given him.*

Oftentimes we see others display a wealth of knowledge in particular area of life. Some persons even seem to know what to do in every situation. We look at them in awe and refer to them as wise. Would you like to be wise? You can be. Wisdom belongs to God. He gives it. Wisdom is not only for some people, it is for everyone. If you do not have any or if you need more, ask God for it. God answers our prayers. He will give you wisdom in large amounts. He will give you liberally. God is not stingy with the wisdom which he gives. So, resolve to pray for wisdom every day for the remainder of your life.

PRAYER: Lord, today I ask You for wisdom. I need wisdom for daily living - in my studies, in my relationship with my parents and friends. Please help me to understand the things I read and the instructions my teachers give me, in Jesus' name, amen.

DAY 55

SEPTEMBER 24

God Keeps His Promises

Genesis 13:16; 22:17 (KJV)

> *And I will make thy seed as the dust of the earth: so that if a man can number the dust of the earth, then shall thy seed also be numbered.*

> *That in blessing I will bless thee, and in multiplying I will multiply thy seed as the stars of the heaven, and as the sand which is upon the sea shore; and thy seed shall possess the gate of his enemies;*

1 Kings 4:20 (KJV)

> *Judah and Israel were many, as the sand which is by the sea in multitude, eating and drinking, and making merry.*

God promised Abraham that he would make his offsprings as numerous as the sand of the seashore. Imagine that! People as many as the sands of the seashore. And, to think that all those persons can be traced back to one man – Abraham! Although the thought is mindboggling and to the natural mind it seems impossible, God made that promise to Abraham and He kept His promise. Descendants of Abraham are still being born today. They will continue to be born until the day Jesus returns. God is faithful. Whatever He has promises you, He will bring every to pass in your life.

CONFESSION: God keeps His promises. No matter how impossible a promise seems, nothing is impossible to God therefore, I patiently wait to see the manifestation of His promises in my life.

DAY 56

SEPTEMBER 25

Develop Your Gift

Proverbs 18:16 (KJV)

> *A man's gift makes room for him and brings him before great men.*

You have a natural ability to do something. It may be track and field, singing, playing the piano, baking, painting or doing business. Even though you have a natural ability, there are techniques that you will need to develop to perfect your talent or ability. These techniques are developed through practice. Will you schedule time to practice those techniques? As you practice you will receive guidance from a coach or mentor. Will you listen to and apply the advice of that person? Decide to be disciplined enough to develop your gift because one day that gift will take you before great men. On that day you should be excellent. Excellence comes through practice, through repetition.

PRAYER: Lord, please help me to develop my gifts, talents and abilities. Let excellence be the minimum standard in my life in Jesus name, amen.

DAY 57

SEPTEMBER 26

Do It in Anticipation

1 Kings 7:14 (KJV)

> *He was a widow's son of the tribe of Naphtali, and his father was a man of Tyre, a worker in brass: and he was filled with wisdom, and understanding, and cunning to work all works in brass. And he came to king Solomon, and wrought all his work.*

While at school you are discovering and developing your skills and talents. Take the time to work at perfecting them. When you take the time to develop your skills and talents, to become exceptionally good at what you do, kings and other high ranking leaders will send for you. They will commission your work. They will engage your services. School is preparation time for a great future. Life is waiting to celebrate your skills and talents. Do not shortchange yourself of the opportunity to be great by being lazy. Do not stand in the way of your destiny. Dedicate yourself to the rigours of learning. You will not regret it.

CONFESSION: By the grace of God I will develop and perfect my skills and talents through practice. I will have a good attitude to those who provide instruction about how to develop them.

DAY 58

SEPTEMBER 27

It Starts With Fearing God

Proverbs 9:10 (KJV)

> *The fear of the LORD is the beginning of wisdom: and the knowledge of the holy is understanding.*

The starting point to gaining wisdom is having reverence for God, fearing Him. Today many person refer to God in ways that are far less than reverential. The tone they use when speaking to and of God makes one wonder whether they are aware of His sovereignty. Do not descend into disrespectful behavior towards God. Your actions and speech should always be respectful of Him. God is to be held in high esteem. He is to be honoured. Only a fool would not reverence God. If a person does not reverence God he cannot claim to be wise. Therefore, know that by fearing God you have positioned yourself at the first stage of acquiring wisdom. When you have a knowledge of God you are able to filter all your experiences through your knowledge of Him therefore, your understanding will be astounding to many.

PRAYER: Lord, please teach me to fear You. Help me to gain a thorough understanding of You in Jesus name, amen.

DAY 59

SEPTEMBER 28

A Signpost

1 Kings 10:9 (KJV)

> *Blessed be the LORD thy God, which delighted in thee, to set thee on the throne of Israel: because the LORD loved Israel for ever, therefore made he thee king, to do judgment and justice.*

When the Queen of Sheba met King Solomon she said his wisdom and prosperity was in excess of what she had been told. She recognized that his wisdom and riches were the blessing of God and not of his own efforts. You are a Christian in a school with many children; can they look at your life and see the blessing of God? Can your classmates acknowledge the existence of God because of what they see in your life?: (St. Matthew 5:16). God's blessings may not always look like physical prosperity but certainly God's character - His wisdom, knowledge and love – which is part of the blessing, should be reflected in you.

CONFESSION: I will live my life so that others will see the blessings of God in me and on me.

DAY 60

SEPTEMBER 29

Treasure Your Inheritance

1 Kings 21:1-3 (KJV)

> *And it came to pass after these things, that Naboth the Jezreelite had a vineyard, which was in Jezreel, hard by the palace of Ahab king of Samaria.*
>
> *And Ahab spake unto Naboth, saying, Give me thy vineyard, that I may have it for a garden of herbs, because it is near unto my house: and I will give thee for it a better vineyard than it; or, if it seem good to thee, I will give thee the worth of it in money.*
>
> *And Naboth said to Ahab, The Lord forbid it me, that I should give the inheritance of my fathers unto thee.*

King Ahab coveted Naboth's vineyard and invited him to sell it or exchange it for a better piece of land but Naboth refused because the vineyard had been passed down through his family for many generations. What a blessing Naboth came into! Someone took the Word of God seriously and left an inheritance for His greatgrandchildren!: (See Prov. 3: 22). King Ahab wanted to plant a herb garden on the land. Herbs are not enduring plants. A herb garden could have been planted almost anywhere but King Ahab simply wanted the convenience that that particular plot offered – it was near his house. Naboth, full of wisdom and understanding the importance of the land in his family, refused to sell or exchange it. What items or lessons have been passed down to you through your parents that you should preserve because it is a valuable legacy? Do not part with what had been passed down to you to satisfy someone's fleeting whims. Preserve your family's good and Godly legacy.

DECLARATION: I will keep my inheritance. I will not exchange it. I will not part with it.

SEPTEMBER 30

Discovering the Bible

2 Kings 22:8-11 (KJV)

> *And Hilkiah the high priest said unto Shaphan the scribe, I have found the book of the law in the house of the LORD. And Hilkiah gave the book to Shaphan, and he read it.*
>
> *And Shaphan the scribe came to the king, and brought the king word again, and said, Thy servants have gathered the money that was found in the house, and have delivered it into the hand of them that do the work, that have the oversight of the house of the LORD.*
>
> *And Shaphan the scribe shewed the king, saying, Hilkiah the priest hath delivered me a book. And Shaphan read it before the king.*
>
> *And it came to pass, when the king had heard the words of the book of the law, that he rent his clothes.*

Sometimes we sin against God because we do not know what He requires. You have to read the Bible to know what God wants you to do or not do. When you become aware of what God requires; if you were doing wrong, you are to ask His forgiveness and immediately stop doing that thing or those things. You should also do the same in school: when you realize that an action is in violation of the school rules you should stop doing it immediately. In the same way, when you realize that a habit will cause you to get low grades you should stop doing it and do what will cause your grades to improve.

PRAYER: Lord, please give me the grace to read and understand Your Word. Please give me grace to read and understand my textbooks. It is through reading that ignorance will be changed to knowledge. I thank You for that grace in Jesus name, amen.

DAY 62

OCTOBER 1

1 Chronicles 4: 9-19 (KJV)

> *And Jabez was more honourable than his brethren: and his mother called his name Jabez, saying, Because I bare him with sorrow.*
>
> *And Jabez called on the God of Israel, saying, Oh that thou wouldest bless me indeed, and enlarge my coast, and that thine hand might be with me, and that thou wouldest keep me from evil, that it may not grieve me! And God granted him that which he requested.*

The circumstances of your birth do not matter. If you ask God to change your future He will. Just look at Jabez, each time someone called his name he was reminded of the sorrow his mother experienced at his birth. However, he asked God to make things different and God did. If you want God to change your story, pray the prayer of Jabez.

PRAYER: Oh that thou wouldest bless me indeed, and enlarge my coast, and that thine hand might be with me, and that thou wouldest keep me from evil, that it may not grieve me. In Jesus name, amen.

DAY 63

OCTOBER 2

Surpassing Their Limitations

1 Chronicles 11:5 (KJV)

> *And the inhabitants of Jebus said to David, Thou shalt not come hither. Nevertheless David took the castle of Zion, which is the city of David.*

People will tell you how far you can go in life, what you can become and what you will or will not be able to do however; the extent of your achievements is entirely up to you. Though the Jebusites tried to limit how far David could go he did not allow their words to define his progress. Instead he defied them and took the castle. Will you defy the negative words and become all that you were created to be?

DECLARATION: My achievements in life are limited only by the Word of God. I will become all that God created me to be.

DAY 64

OCTOBER 3

Appearance

St. Matthew 6:28-29 (KJV)

> *And why take ye thought for raiment? Consider the lilies of the field, how they grow; they toil not, neither do they spin:*
>
> *And yet I say unto you, That even Solomon in all his glory was not arrayed like one of these.*
>
> *Wherefore, if God so clothe the grass of the field, which today is, and tomorrow is cast into the oven, shall he not much more clothe you, O ye of little faith?*

You are at the stage of life where your appearance really matters. How you dress has become very important to you. During adolescence there can be much pressure to wear the latest fashion at all times however, some persons may not be able to. If you find yourself in that situation or if your best is a second-hand garment, wear it proudly and without shame. Always ensure that your clothes are washed and neatly ironed. Remember that you are created in God's image. He clothe the lilies - delicately beautiful and short-lived flowers. Imagine what He will do for you! Do not despair. Know that God has clothed you and someday you will be able wear better clothing. If you know someone who is not always able to wear fashionable clothing, do not make fun of him or her. Do not make that person feel uncomfortable. Let your appreciation for that person go beyond the garment that is worn.

CONFESSION: I will be satisfied with the clothing that I have until God provides more or better. I will appreciate others for who they are and not what they wear.

DAY 65

OCTOBER 4

Discerning The Times

1 Chronicles 12:32 (KJV)

And of the children of Issachar, which were men that had understanding of the times, to know what Israel ought to do; the heads of them were two hundred; and all their brethren were at their commandment.

There are seasons of nature – spring, summer, autumn, winter. There are seasons of life – childhood, adolescence and adulthood. You may be leaving childhood and is on the verge of adolescence or you may be smacked in the middle of adolescence. In this season you are in school. You are to be learning. It is the season in which you begin to lay the foundation for your life. You are studying to pass examinations so that you can matriculate for college or university and read for a diploma or degree, after which you will enter a trade, career or profession. Ask God to help you to better understand the season that you are in. Also ask Him to help you understand what is required in your current season of life. Knowing what to do in each season was a gift that the children of Issachar had. If you get this gift, you will also know what to do in each season. This knowledge will help you to avoid some of the pains and pitfalls of life. If you do not make the necessary preparation in one season you will be at a disadvantage in the next season.

PRAYER: Father God, please help me to discern and understand the seasons of life. Help me to do all that is required of me in each season in Jesus name, amen.

OCTOBER 5

The Presence of God

1 Chronicles 13:14 (KJV)

> *And the ark of God remained with the family of Obededom
> in his house three months. And the LORD blessed the house of
> Obededom, and all that he had.*

Because the presence of God was in Obededom's house God blessed his entire family. Whenever someone creates space for God to reside, He is sure to bless the occupants of that place. By waking up early for Family Bible Hour, your parents are creating a space in your home for God to dwell. Do not resent the fact that your parents insist that you attend Family Bible Hour. Get together with your family and help to create a space and an atmosphere where the presence of God can come and dwell. God will bless you and your family as He did Obededom's household.

CONFESSION: I will participate in Family Bible Hour. I will help to create an atmosphere in my home in which God can dwell.

DAY 67

OCTOBER 6

Humility

Job 9:4 (KJV)

> *He is wise in heart, and mighty in strength: who hath*
> *hardened himself against him, and hath prospered?*

God is infinitely wise. He is mighty – He is able to do all that He says and intends to do. There is no limit to His power. God is great, just and awesomely powerful. If a person decides to try to resist God, he will not succeed. A person cannot fight against God and prosper. Therefore, humble yourself before the almighty God. Yield to Him. Be at peace with Him. Read and obey His word. Prosperity comes by submitting to God and aligning yourself with His will and His word.

PRAYER: Lord help me not to fight against You as You know what's best for me. You are mighty and strong and all wise.

DAY 68

OCTOBER 7

In A Class by Himself

1 Chronicles 17:20 (KJV)

> *O Lord, there is none like thee, neither is there any God beside thee, according to all that we have heard with our ears.*

There is no god like I Am That I Am. Jehovah is God. He existed before the earth was formed. He alone is God. True worshippers always acknowledge and declare the uniqueness and sovereignty of God. Since you have been born, have you heard of any other that equals or rivals God? Surely not! God is above all others. He is in a class by Himself so we declare that He is Lord. There is none like Him and there is none beside Him. There will never be any like Him or beside Him.

DECLARATION: There is no other god beside God, the Creator of heaven and earth.

DAY 69

OCTOBER 8

None Beside Him

Isaiah 44:6 (KJV)

> *Thus saith the LORD the King of Israel, and his redeemer the
> LORD of hosts; I am the first, and I am the last; and beside
> me there is no God.*

True worshippers declare that there is none beside God. They declare that none can rival Him. However, there is an even better testimony of God's sovereignty. God knows all things. He created the heaven and earth. He knows the name of every star. He was before time. He created time and called it into existence. He knows all things. Who would successfully dispute the testimony of such an authoritative person? God who knows everything says He is the only God – "beside me there is no God". No one can successfully dispute God's testimony.

CONFESSION: You are Lord, O God. I trust Your purpose and direction for my life. You know all things so please help me to trust Your sovereignty.

DAY 70

OCTOBER 9

To My Rescue

2 Chronicles 16:9(a) (KJV)

> *For the eyes of the LORD run to and fro throughout the whole earth, to shew himself strong in the behalf of them whose heart is perfect toward him.*

The Holy Spirit, the Spirit of God, is looking in the earth for persons whose hearts are perfect towards God. What does it mean to have a heart that is perfect towards God? It is to be committed to God; walking in obedience and untainted faith as He directs. Remember Abraham? He had a promise from God – God was going to give him a son. God then told him to walk before Him and be blameless or perfect (Gen. 17:1). Later, God instructed Abraham to sacrifice the manifested promise, His son (Gen. 22:1-2). Today the Holy Spirit is looking throughout the whole earth for such persons. Are you sincere towards God? Will you submit to Him without question? Will you have faith in Him? Will you trust Him? If your heart is not perfect towards God, resolve to have that heart and work towards it.

PRAYER: Lord, I acknowledge that there is none as great as You. Thank You that the Holy Spirit is looking throughout the earth for persons whose hearts are perfect towards You. I want to be such a person. I want the Holy Spirit to show Himself strong on my behalf. So, Lord today I ask for Your help in becoming a person whose heart is perfect towards You.

DAY 71

OCTOBER 10

Light and Protection

Psalm 84:11(AMP)

> *For the Lord God is a Sun and Shield; the Lord bestows*
> *[present] grace and favor and [future] glory (honor, splendor,*
> *and heavenly bliss)! No good thing will He withhold from*
> *those who walk uprightly.*

When you trust God He will give you all the things that are necessary for life. He is a Sun and a Shield. The sun gives light which is necessary for life. A shield protects you from injury which could be caused by the enemy's weapon. God does not withhold anything good from His people who walk uprightly - are honest and have high moral standards. Is a great report card a great thing? Is excelling in extra-curricular activity a good thing? God will help you to achieve them if you walk uprightly.

PRAYER: Lord, today I bless you because You provide for me. Help me to always remember that You will not withhold any good thing from those who are honest and have high moral standards.

DAY 72

OCTOBER 11

Look to God Always

2 Chronicles 20:12 (KJV)

O our God, wilt thou not judge them? for we have no might against this great company that cometh against us; neither know we what to do: but our eyes are upon thee.

Oftentimes we start towards our goals with excitement and great anticipation however, along the way the requirements of achievement become overwhelming. Your studies can become overwhelming. You look at all the assignments that are due within the same period as the several tests that you must take. If you reach the point where you do not know what to do, turn your eyes upon God. Look to Him. Breathe. Sometimes a one word prayer is all you need to pray - "Help!" God will help you. Do not remain silent.

CONFESSION: No matter how overwhelming my studies become I know that God will help me through.

DAY 73

OCTOBER 12

2 Chronicles 34:1-2 (KJV)

> *Josiah was eight years old when he began to reign, and he reigned in Jerusalem one and thirty years.*
>
> *And he did that which was right in the sight of the LORD, and walked in the ways of David his father, and declined neither to the right hand, nor to the left.*

Josiah was eight years old when he became king of Israel. That is a very young age to have the responsibilities and expectations of an entire country thrust on anyone. However, Josiah did not allow his age to be an excuse for failure or to do silly things. Instead he walked in the way of his father David – he emulated what David did. David was known to be in communication with God. He was a worshipper who always sought God to the point where God said David was a man after His own heart (1 Sam. 13:14, Acts 13:22). You are not too young for leadership. As a class monitor, student counsellor or peer counsellor you are a leader. Will you do as Josiah did? Will you walk in the Godly way of your father, your mother, your grandmother, grandfather?

PRAYER: Lord, I thank You for people who show me Your ways by their actions. Please help me to follow after their example and do the things that are right in Your sight in Jesus' name, amen.

DAY 74

OCTOBER 13

Isaiah 58:6 (KJV)

Is not this the fast that I have chosen? To loose the bands of wickedness, to undo the heavy burdens, and to let the oppressed go free, and that ye break every yoke?

Fasting is very important to your spiritual growth. When you fast, please ensure that it is a true fast. This means that you use the time of abstinence from food to seek God in prayer. Engaging in a true fast will help you develop self-control. A true fast also guarantees many spiritual blessings: (See Isaiah 58:7-14). Can you identify the twenty blessings of a true fast from the text?

CHALLENGE: Make plans to join the next fast that your church plans. Be sure to pray and read the Bible while you fast.

OCTOBER 14

Seek God Through Fasting

Ezra 8:21 (KJV)

> *Then I proclaimed a fast there, at the river of Ahava, that we might afflict ourselves before our God, to seek of him a right way for us, and for our little ones, and for all our substance.*

The children of Israel had been taken captive by the Babylonians. They were returning home under the leadership of Ezra. On the second trip Ezra stopped so that the children of Israel could fast and pray to God for protection from the enemies who were waiting to attack them along the way. God heard their prayer and saw their fast. He answered and took them safely to Jerusalem. You too should seek God's guidance, protection and provision through prayer and fasting.

CONFESSION: I will seek God's protection and provision through the principles of prayer and fasting.

DAY 76

OCTOBER 15

Favour to Rebuild

Nehemiah 2:10 (KJV)

> *When Sanballat the Horonite, and Tobiah the servant, the Ammonite, heard of it, it grieved them exceedingly that there was come a man to seek the welfare of the children of Israel.*

Nehemiah was an Israelite who was taken into captivity by the Babylonians. He worked for the king of Babylon and was one of the leaders who took the Israelites back to Judah. Before starting the journey back, Nehemiah prayed to God that the king of Babylon would give him favour and God answered his prayer. When Nehemiah asked the king's permission to rebuild his fathers' sepulture the king gave him letters guaranteeing his safe journey to Judah. However, when Sanballat and Tobiah heard about Nehemiah's request and the king's response they were very upset. Their distress was caused by the fact that Nehemiah had taken the initiative to speak to the king about a matter that was good for Israel. If you aspire to restore your family's standing or fortune and you meet opposition, do not be discouraged. Keep trying. Ask God for favour and He will make you find it with the right people.

CONFESSION: I will not be put off by people who are upset with my efforts to make the lives of others better. God will give me favour with who I need it.

DAY 77

OCTOBER 16

Obedience Results In Favour

Esther 2:15 (KJV)

> *Now when the turn for Esther the daughter of Abihail, the uncle of Mordecai who had taken her as his own daughter, had come to go in to the king, she required nothing but what Hegai the king's attendant, the keeper of the women, suggested. And Esther won favor in the sight of all who saw her.*

It is important to follow instructions and listen to your teachers. During the preparation period, Esther required nothing except what Hegai, the king's attendant suggested. Her obedience caused her to be favoured in the sight of all. Isn't it interesting that obedience can cause you to be favoured by others? Teachers know what you need and what you do not need. If you are willing, they will gladly instruct you to become the best you can be. Observe, listen and follow instructions. In this way you will obtain favour from all who you interact with.

PRAYER: Lord help me to follow the instructions of those in authority. Open my mind to receive wisdom from my teachers and cause me to excel in Jesus' name. Amen

DAY 78

OCTOBER 17

Command the Morning

Job 38:2 (KJV)

> *Who is this that darkens counsel [questioning my authority and wisdom] By words without knowledge? (AMP)*

Sometime we are presumptuous in the way we speak of God and His government. In the doubting and the questioning, God reminded Job of who He is. In the same way that God questioned Job to highlight his ignorance, so too are we to question ourselves. May you never speak about God from a place of ignorance.

DECLARATION: The Lord is sovereign. He is above all else. I will always be mindful of who God is. I will always speak with that knowledge in mind. I salute the Lord God of heaven.

OCTOBER 18

Standing Solo

Romans 11:2-4 (KJV)

> *God hath not cast away his people which he foreknew. Wot ye not what the scripture saith of Elias? how he maketh intercession to God against Israel saying,*
>
> *Lord, they have killed thy prophets, and digged down thine altars; and I am left alone, and they seek my life.*
>
> *But what saith the answer of God unto him? I have reserved to myself seven thousand men, who have not bowed the knee to the image of Baal.*

Sometimes standing for God can feel lonely. Do you ever feel like you are the only one in your home, school or community that is standing for God? Elias felt the same way and he spoke to God about it. God assured him that there were seven thousand men who were also standing for Him. Elias was not alone. Take heart. God's response to Elias them is the same to you today. You are not the only one standing for God and one day you will meet a great company who has also decided to stand for Him.

PRAYER: Lord, give me grace to do what is right in Your sight. Even when I feel like I am the only one being faithful to You help me to remember that there are others, even if they are not in my immediate environment.

DAY 80

OCTOBER 19

The Blessed Man

Psalm 1:1-2 (KJV)

> *Blessed is the man that walketh not in the counsel of the ungodly, nor standeth in the way of sinners, nor sitteth in the seat of the scornful.*

> *But his delight is in the law of the LORD; and in his law doth he meditate day and night.*

There is a blessing for those who do not take advice from or follow the plans of ungodly people. There is also a blessing for the person who does not stand submissively among sinner or go to sit for relaxation where scornful people gather. The blessed man takes pleasure in God's laws, in His instructions and commandments. He also thinks about God's laws during the day and at night. Who do you ask for advice? Are your advisors Godly? Do you socialize with those who mock other Christians and speak negatively about God?

CHALLENGE: Will you emulate the blessed man? Will you become the blessed man?

DAY 81

OCTOBER 20

Awaken By His Goodness

Psalm 3:5 (AMP)

> *I lay down and slept; I wakened again, for the Lord sustains me.*

Oftentimes we go to sleep with no care in the world and we awake the next morning without a thought of the goodness of God. Sleep is said to be the closest thing to death. Some people go to sleep and never awaken. Whenever you awaken from sleep it is a good time to give God thanks as you have no ability to awaken yourself from sleep. God keeps you during sleep and you only awake because of His goodness.

PRAYER: Lord, I am grateful for another day. Thank You for protecting me while I slept. Thank You for allowing me to wake up. Thank you for life. In Jesus name I pray, amen.

DAY 82

OCTOBER 21

Blessings of the Righteous

Psalm 5:11-12 (KJV)

> *But let all those that put their trust in thee rejoice: let them*
> *ever shout for joy, because thou defendest them: let them also*
> *that love thy name be joyful in thee.*
>
> *For thou, Lord, wilt bless the righteous; with favour wilt*
> *thou compass him as with a shield.*

Here we see that there are five blessings to those who trust God, love Him and love His name. Such persons have a refuge (place of safety) in Him. They are joyful in Him. They have security in Him. They are blessed of Him. They have His favour. If you trust God, love Him and love His name then you are assured of these blessing.

PRAYER: Father, please help me to love You and Your name with all my being. Father I want to trust You unconditionally.

DAY 83

OCTOBER 22

Pure Words

Psalm 12:6 (KJV)

The words of the LORD are pure words: as silver tried in a furnace of earth, purified seven times.

There is no impurity in God's Word. His words are purified of all impurities and falsehoods. God's Words has been tried in fire. His promises are firm, His commandments are without ambiguity, the gospel is untainted. The words of God has stood the test of time therefore, we can trust in them completely. If you do as His Word says you will have more than a bankable proposal. You will have exponential returns at all times. God's Words will not fail you. His Word has never failed anyone who fulfilled the terms.

PRAYER: Lord, thank You for Your Word. Please help me to believe Your Word. Please help me to allow Your Word to guide me.

DAY 84

OCTOBER 23

The Path of Life

Psalm 16:11 (KJV)

Thou wilt shew me the path of life: in thy presence is fullness of joy; at thy right hand there are pleasures for evermore.

The path of life is Jesus Christ. There is no other person on earth that you can call on or go through to receive eternal life. Jesus opened the way to salvation by dying on the cross at Calvary and raising on the third day. Christ, our risen Saviour is seated at God's right hand where there is everlasting joy in its purest form. At God's right hand there are pleasures in perpetuity. Accept Christ, the path of life; the only way to heaven where you will experience everlasting joy. Today is a good day to begin on the path of life. Pray the following prayer:

Lord, I have sinned. I repent of my sins. Jesus, please come into my heart and save me. I believe you died on the cross for my sins; that you rose from the dead and is now seated at God's right hand. Please live in my heart forever. Fill me with the Holy Spirit. Thank You for saving me, amen

CONFESSION: Jesus is the only way to God, to eternal life.

DAY 85

OCTOBER 24

No Money Necessary

Isaiah 55:1 (KJV)

> *Ho, every one that thirsteth, come ye to the waters, and he*
> *that hath no money; come ye, buy, and eat; yea, come, buy*
> *wine and milk without money and without price.*

Jesus made provision for everyone to have salvation. He recognized that if it was sold some persons would not be able to afford it. You do not need money to get salvation because it is free. When Jesus died at Calvary he paid the price for our salvation and thereby made it free. The free gift of salvation is available to all. The only requirement is that persons come, that they accept the gift. All are welcome to the blessings of salvation.

CHALLENGE: Share this truth with someone today.

PRAYER: Lord please forgive me of my sins, take my burdens and grant me Your presence.

DAY 86

OCTOBER 25

Love Unlimited

John 3:16 (KJV)

> *For God so loved the world, that he gave his only begotten*
> *Son, that whosoever believeth in him should not perish, but*
> *have everlasting life.*

Jesus died so that all persons can be saved. Do not assume that the persons sitting on your left and your right, in front of and behind you have heard about Jesus. Do not assume that they because they speak Christianese they have accepted His gift of salvation. Why not share the gospel with all who you meet today? If you have never accepted Jesus as Saviour please do so now by saying the following prayer:

> *Lord, I have sinned. I repent of my sins. Jesus, please come*
> *into my heart and save me. I believe you died on the cross*
> *for my sins; that you rose from the dead and is now seated*
> *at God's right hand. Please live in my heart forever. Fill me*
> *with the Holy Spirit. Thank You for saving me, amen.*

CHALLENGE: Share the gospel with every person you meet.

DAY 87

OCTOBER 26

Committed To Love

Psalm 18:1 (KJV)

I will love thee, O Lᴏʀᴅ, my strength.

David loved God ardently. This is seen from his vow to love God. In professing his intent, David recognized the Lord as the source of his strength. How do you feel towards God when you recount his goodness and mercies towards you? Do you love God? Take a minute and consider the question before answering.

CHALLENGE: If your answer is yes, pray for grace to continue loving Him. If your answer is no, will you vow to love God.

PRAYER: O for grace to keep loving You Lord.

DAY 88

OCTOBER 27

Multifaceted God

Psalm 18:2 (KJV)

> *The LORD is my rock, and my fortress, and my deliverer; my God, my strength, in whom I will trust; my buckler, and the horn of my salvation, and my high tower.*

David had to run to escape King Saul's malice fuelled wrath. When David fled he found safety in the mountains. After this experience David identified and compared God with the safety that the mountains provided. God is that place of safety and concealment for you today. Whatever terror pursues you, run to God who is a fortress and a deliverer. He is solid, unchanging, and strong. You can exercise your faith in Him. From the passage you will see that God was eight things God to David. He is those things to you too.

DECLARATION: Make your declaration based on the verse.

OCTOBER 28

Perfect God

Psalm 18:30 (KJV)

As for God, his way is perfect: the word of the LORD is tried:
he is a buckler to all those that trust in him.

God's character is astounding. His doings are perfect. There is no fault with the method by which He does things. His Word has been tested throughout time and has been found to be all that it promised to be. God is a weapon of war for those who have confident expectation in Him. Imagine that! God is a buckler - a small shield worn on the forearm - for those who trust in Him. Indeed His way is perfect. Blessed be God.

PRAYER: Lord I thank You that Your way is perfect, that Your Word has been tested and tried and has been proven to be true. I thank You that Your Word provides me with protection because I trust in You.

OCTOBER 29

Declaring His Glory

Psalm 19:1 (KJV)

The heavens declare the glory of God; and the firmament sheweth his handywork.

Creation acknowledges and confirms the magnificence of God. The heavens, the earth and the seas show the intricacy, creativity and mastery of His work. The firmament shows God's skillful workmanship. Even if some men deny God, creation - the intricate workmanship of nature - will always point back to Him. Creation is a School of Divinity.

CONFESSION: Creation declares God's glory. When I look at creation I am compelled to acknowledge and declare God's glory.

DAY 91

OCTOBER 30

Perfect Word

Psalm 19: 7 (KJV)

> *The law of the LORD is perfect, converting the soul: the testimony of the LORD is sure, making wise the simple.*

The doctrine of God is perfect, it is without fault. It has the ability to restore any person who has sinned. Whatever God testifies of is sure. There is no mistake in His testimony. When we are humble and teachable His Word will make us wise and enlightened. It is through this process that fallen men are able to accept salvation. The perfect Word of God has the ability to do what you are incapable of doing for yourself.

CHALLENGE: Read through verse 19 and identify the six blessings of the Word.

DAY 92

OCTOBER 31

Psalm 24:6 (KJV)

> *This is the generation of them that seek him, that seek thy face, O Jacob. Selah.*

There is a generation whose hands are clean and whose hearts are pure. This generation does not trust in idols or swear by false gods. The people of that generation seek the Lord with their whole heart. Do not be left out. You are a part of the generation that is seeking God's face. Choose to participate. Seek the Lord with all that you are.

DECLARATION: I will seek God through reading His Word, praying and fasting, reading anointed books and listening to recorded messages from His ministers.

DAY 93

NOVEMBER 1

Bless the Lord!

Psalm 34:1 (KJV)

> *I will bless the LORD at all times: his praise shall continually be in my mouth.*

Praise is the staple of knowing God. David, an avid and widely admired worshipper, vowed to praise God at all times. Challenge yourself to praising God at all times for seven days and journal your experiences.

DECLARATION: I will bless the Lord at all times.

DAY 94

NOVEMBER 2

Pleasure in His Servant's Prosperity

Psalm 35:27 (KJV)

> *Let them shout for joy, and be glad, that favour my righteous cause: yea, let them say continually, Let the LORD be magnified, which hath pleasure in the prosperity of his servant.*

Imagine that! God takes pleasure in the prosperity of his servants. A servant is a person who performs duties for others. He or she is a person employed in a household to carry out domestic duties. Many persons frown upon being called a servant, even a servant of the Most High God. However, this is the most distinguished role that you can have on earth. Are you God's servant? Do you have and carry out any duty in His house? If you are God's servant it is His pleasure to see you prosper, which includes to see you excel in school.

CHALLENGE: Begin to serve in the church you attend.

DAY 95

NOVEMBER 3

Fruit of the Spirit

Galatians 5:22-23 (KJV)

> *But the fruit of the Spirit is love, joy, peace, longsuffering, gentleness, goodness, faith,*
>
> *Meekness, temperance: against such there is no law.*

As you grow in Jesus you will begin to see the manifestation of the fruit of the spirit in your life. You will see love, joy, peace, longsuffering, gentleness, goodness, faith, meekness and temperance. There is no law against a person being loving, joyful, peaceful, forgiving and selfless, gentle, good, faithful, meek and temperate. Such character traits are the natural product of the Holy Spirit at work in a child of God. Are you seeing the fruit of the spirit in your life? What is absent? What needs to be developed? Ask the Holy Spirit to help you.

PRAYER: Lord, I thank You that as I grow in Jesus the fruit of the Spirit also grows in my life.

DAY 96

NOVEMBER 4

Pleasure in God

Psalm 37:4 (KJV)

> *Delight thyself also in the LORD: and he shall give thee the desires of thine heart.*

Take great pleasure in God. Enjoy Him. If you are an ice-cream or a chocolate lover you understand the joy that the thought of having a cone or a piece of chocolate brings. Just as some things bring you joy, make God the joy of your heart. When you do this He will give you the things that you are to desire: He will place desires in your heart. After placing desires in your heart God will also fulfill them. How super awesome is that?!

CONFESSION: I delight myself in God.

DAY 97

NOVEMBER 5

Commit Your Goals

Psalm 37:5 (KJV)

> *Commit thy way unto the LORD; trust also in him; and he shall bring it to pass.*

Whatever desire God has placed in your heart He will cause it to come true, to materialize. When you commit the path that you will take in achieving your goals to God, He will make a way for those goals to be accomplished. For instant, if He places the desire in your heart to become an architect He will make all provision for you to achieve that goal. Your job is commit the path to Him and trust in Him as you take the journey.

PRAYER: Lord I commit _____ to You. I trust you to bring it/them to pass.

NOVEMBER 6

Ordered Steps

Psalm 37:23 (KJV)

> *The steps of a good man are ordered by the LORD: and he delighteth in his way.*

The Lord directs each step that a good man takes. He guides, supports and establishes every one of them whether it be in relation to spiritual or earthly things. Sometimes God does not show His servant the entire picture - a promise is made and you must trust Him to take you into it, one step at a time. You must confidently know God will show you where to go and the method(s) to use. When you follows God's direction you will achieve success.

PRAYER: Lord please order my steps. May the Holy Spirit always lead me to do good, in Jesus name, amen.

DAY 99

NOVEMBER 7

Show Favour

Psalm 112:5 (KJV)

> *A good man sheweth favour, and lendeth: he will guide his*
> *affairs with discretion.*

The teenage years is a period when children become mean to others because they want to fit in a group or because they do not think that a peer is pretty enough or good enough. A good person is kind to others and hopes for nothing in return. A good person is also prudent and frugal. He is economical in his affairs and is able to lend to those who are in need. In this way he helps someone meet their immediate needs and those of others. Today, make the decision to be a good person by showing favour to others.

DECLARATION: In my interaction with my peers I will be generous and kind. I will lend to others. I will think about justice and do what is just in everything I do.

DAY 100

NOVEMBER 8

Burden Bearer

Luke 6:38 (KJV)

> *Give, and it shall be given unto you; good measure, pressed down, and shaken together, and running over, shall men give into your bosom. For with the same measure that ye mete withal it shall be measured to you again.*

One of the characteristics of God's children is generosity. It is important to show limitless kindness to everyone, especially the poor and destitute. If you have a giving spirit you will reap the benefit. Whatever you give - money, mercy, kindness – will come back to you in a larger quantity. Likewise, if you give sparingly the return will be small when compared to what it would be if you gave generously.

CHALLENGE: Give something, in a large quantity, today.

NOVEMBER 9

Sustainer

Psalm 55:22 (KJV)

> *Cast thy burden upon the LORD, and he shall sustain thee: he shall never suffer the righteous to be moved.*

What burdens you? Whatever it is, God has promised that if you throw it on Him He will sustain you, that is, He will strengthen you - support you physically and mentally as you pray for His mercy and grace. Close your eyes and visualize yourself throwing everything that burdens you on God. Now, be confident in the knowledge that they are with God and He will do with them as He pleases.

PRAYER: Lord, I thank You that I can unload my burdens on You and You will sustain me.

DAY 102

NOVEMBER 10

The Beatitudes

St. Matthew 5: 3 (KJV)

> *Blessed are the poor in spirit: for theirs is the kingdom of heaven.*

Jesus' teaching on the mountain is called The Beatitudes. Beatitudes are verses in the Bible beginning with the word 'blessed'. You will note that the verses of St. Matthew 5:3-11 begin with the word 'blessed'. Here Jesus stated the ideal character of His followers. They are poor in spirit, they mourn over sin and its effect upon people, they are self-controlled, they crave righteousness, they show mercy to the poor and needy, they are pure in heart, they make peace with and between men, they are persecuted because of their righteous – Godly – ways, and they are persecuted and reproached by men for Christ's sake.

CHALLENGE: Memorize each of the beatitudes. Examine yourself to see whether you have any of the characteristics of the blessed.

DAY 103

NOVEMBER 11

Answer Softly

Proverbs 15:1 (KJV)

> *A soft answer turneth away wrath: but grievous words stir*
> *up anger.*

Our society has socialized you to either withdraw in a sullen manner or respond in a way that mirrors a threat. However, you have to re-socialize yourself to give a response when threatened. Your response should be below the threat level. Can you imagine what will happen if you do not do this? Imagine what happens when you pour fuel on fire. Yes, it erupts into uncontrollable flames. Often the consequences cost more than you are willing to or can pay. Answer. Answer softly.

Prayer: Lord, please help me to answer softly.

DAY 104

NOVEMBER 12

Love Indiscriminately

St. Matthew 5: 43-44 (KJV)

Ye have heard that it hath been said, Thou shalt love thy neighbour, and hate thine enemy.

But I say unto you, Love your enemies, bless them that curse you, do good to them that hate you, and pray for them which despitefully use you, and persecute you

People will do you wrong. Oftentimes you may feel like getting back at those who do you wrong or not like you by saying mean things about them however, you are to do the opposite. There is a higher moral ground that you must take – love them, do good to them and pray for them. It is not easy to pray for someone who has done you wrong but it is possible. Remember that God does not ask us to do the impossible. When you pray for persons who have wronged you, do not ask God to maim or kill them, instead pray that they may encounter the love of God and grow in it.

PRAYER: Lord, please help me to show love to my enemies and bless persons who curse me. Please cause them to experience your love, accept it and grow in it. Help me to also do good to people who hate me. Father, help me to always pray for others who ill-treat me. In Jesus' name I pray, amen.

DAY 105

NOVEMBER 13

Daily Benefits

Psalm 68:19 (KJV)

> *Blessed be the Lord, who daily loadeth us with benefits, even the God of our salvation. Selah.*

Think about it, God provides for you daily. He keeps you. He protects you. He gives you spiritual blessings and earthly ones too. His blessings are benefits and they are many. He gives them to you in large amounts, not in measured quantities. Notice that the verse says He loads you up with benefits? This means that He heaps them upon you. His support for you is always provided so just ask.

PRAYER: Father, thank You for Your daily provision.

DAY 106

NOVEMBER 14

Acknowledge God Now

Ecclesiastes 12:1 (KJV)

> *Remember now thy Creator in the days of thy youth, while the evil days come not, nor the years draw nigh, when thou shalt say, I have no pleasure in them*

Solomon admonishes you to remember God while you are young – when you are in your prime. You are to remember God as your Creator. It is He who brought you into being and who is sustaining you. Solomon advises you not to wait until you are old, afflicted and near death. Remember God today, think about Him. Acknowledge God today and if you haven't already done so, this is a good time to accept the gift of salvation (See Day 86). If you do this, in your old age you will be able to look back at a life well spent working for and worshipping God.

PRAYER: Lord, please help me to always remember You now, while I am young. Help me to remember You before the days of tribulation.

NOVEMBER 15

God My Hope

Psalm 71:5 (KJV)

> *For thou art my hope, O Lord GOD: thou art my trust from my youth.*

David began to trust in God when He was a young man. When he became old he said "I have been young, and now am old; yet have I not seen the righteous forsaken, nor his seed begging bread": (Psalm 37:25 KJV). This is a good testimony of God's faithfulness. Will you also begin to trust God in your youth? How wonderful it would be if in your old age you could share David's testimony by saying 'I have lived from a child, and now am an old man/woman. In that time I have never seen the morally upright abandoned by God. In fact, I have never seen the children of the morally upright begging bread'.

DECLARATION: God is my hope. I choose to trust Him from my youth. I choose to trust Him now.

NOVEMBER 16

I Will Hope in God

Psalm 71:14 (KJV)

> *But I will hope continually, and will yet praise thee more and more.*

To hope means that you have a desire for something specific to happen; you have a feeling of expectation. Being hopeful is important. When a person stops hoping he is likely to remain stagnant. If there is change in his life it is not usually anything to write home about. Hope also means to trust. Trust God continually. Keep hope alive in your life. Keep hoping, keep trusting in God no matter what the situation looks like. As you hope, praise God for whatever you are hoping for.

DECLARATION: I will hope in God continually – at all times throughout the ages.

DAY 109

NOVEMBER 17

Playmaker

Psalm 75:6-7 (KJV)

> *For promotion cometh neither from the east, nor from the west, nor from the south.*
>
> *But God is the judge: he putteth down one, and setteth up another.*

By this time you have heard the phrase, 'It's who you know' used in relation to opportunities or in relation to getting things done. While it is true that persons can open doors and create opportunities for your advancement, do not be depressed if you do not know any human being who can make a way for you. You know God. He is the way maker. He will open doors and create opportunities for you. Do all that is in your power – study hard, study smart, practice – and God will make a way for you to advance.

PRAYER: Father God, I thank You that You will always make a way for me.

DAY 110

NOVEMBER 18

Psalm 84:10 (KJV)

> *For a day in thy courts is better than a thousand. I had rather be a doorkeeper in the house of my God, than to dwell in the tents of wickedness.*

Suppose on the first day of school when you are introducing yourselves to each other one of your classmates says, 'I want to become a doorkeeper'. No doubt the entire class would be shocked. You will agree that being a doorkeeper is not the most prestigious position in any organization. However, as a servant of God it is better to be a doorkeeper at church than to be the Chief Executive Officer of a night club or any other such entity. While you are at school you are still God's servant. Where will you serve? Will you be the person who arrange the chairs for Bible Study or will you be the president of the Mean Girls Club or the Famous Amos Gang?

PRAYER: Lord, I want to be associated with the things that honour You. I want to be in Your house. I prefer do the lowliest job for You than to have a beautiful suite where evil men gather and dwell, in Jesus' name. Amen.

DAY 111

NOVEMBER 19

Crave the Anointing

Psalm 89:20 (KJV)

I have found David My servant; with My holy oil have I anointed him

God anointed David with holy oil. After being anointed David was severely persecuted but none of his persecutors had an advantage over him because God's grace and favour was with him. Later David became King of Israel but he remained submitted to God. He was God's servant. If you are God's servant He will anoint you just as He anointed David. Find somewhere to serve God. Crave the anointing. Ask God to anoint you. His anointing will cause you to excel and succeed.

PRAYER: Lord, please anoint me as You anointed David.

DAY 112

NOVEMBER 20

Number Your Days

Psalm 90:12 (KJV)

> *So teach us to number our days, that we may apply our hearts unto wisdom.*

There is a consequence for every action. Whatever you do today will determine where you are tomorrow, even where you will be five years from today. You will not live forever in this life. God promises us 120 years. There are 43,800 days in 120 years. Will you make each day be one of significance? Let this present day be as your last. Now that you know the number of days in a lifespan of 120 years, will you apply your heart to gaining wisdom?

PRAYER: Lord, help me to always be conscious that I have a set number of days to live and each day that I live is one less. Help me to live each day seeking Your wisdom and doing things that will bring honour and glory to You. I pray in the name of Jesus, amen.

DAY 113

NOVEMBER 21

Anointed With Oil

Psalm 92:10 (KJV)

> *But my horn shalt thou exalt like the horn of an unicorn: I shall be anointed with fresh oil.*

The unicorn's horn represents authority and power. The anointing oil has several mysteries, one of which is to enable ordinary people to perform supernatural things. God's anointing oil strengthens, it enables His children to be triumphant. When you are anointed with fresh oil you are empowered to succeed for God's glory.

CONFESSION: Lord, please anoint me with oil as You did David in Jesus' name, amen.

DAY 114

NOVEMBER 22

Beautiful Me

Song of Solomon 1:5 (KJV)

I am black, but comely, O ye daughters of Jerusalem, as the tents of Kedar, as the curtains of Solomon.

A positive self-image is very important. How you see yourself determines the value you place on yourself (self-esteem) and how much you believe in yourself (self-confidence). You are attractive and agreeable. Look into the mirror and tell yourself how much you admire you, compliment yourself. Sign up to be the first member of your fan club.

DECLARATION: I am beautiful/handsome.

DAY 115

NOVEMBER 23

Perfectly Sculptured

Psalm 139:13-14 (KJV)

> *For thou hast possessed my reins: thou hast covered me in my mother's womb.*
>
> *I will praise thee; for I am fearfully and wonderfully made: marvellous are thy works; and that my soul knoweth right well.*

God has been protecting you from the time you were in your mother's womb. He made you. In this Psalm David acknowledged that God's work in making him is perfect. Does your intellect know that you are perfectly made?

PRAYER: Father God I thank You that I look exactly the way You want me to. You are the master Creator. Your work is incredible. Thank You for taking time to make me.

DAY 116

NOVEMBER 24

I Am The Blessed

Psalm 112:1 (KJV)

> *Praise ye the LORD. Blessed is the man that feareth the LORD,*
> *that delighteth greatly in his commandments.*

Here we see the characteristics of the blessed man. He fears God – he had Godly fear for the Lord and he takes great pleasure in God's commandments. He does what God commands. He keeps God's commandments. Can you identify any characteristics of the blessed man in yourself? These are character traits to develop as God protects and provides for those who fear Him.

DECLARATION: I fear the Lord. I take great pleasure in His commandments. I am the blessed.

DAY 117

NOVEMBER 25

Wealth and Riches

Psalm 112:3 (KJV)

Wealth and riches shall be in his house: and his righteousness endureth for ever.

Wealth and riches are in the house of the blessed man so that his family partakes of it. It is in his posterity. This is the season of life when you learn in preparation to acquire and manage wealth and riches. Prepare well so that you will be able to manage them when they come. The goodness, integrity and uprightness of the good man will last forever.

CONFESSION: I prepare to manage the wealth and riches with which God will entrust to me.

NOVEMBER 26

Called to Be Good

Psalm 112:5 (KJV)

> *A good man sheweth favour, and lendeth: he will guide his affairs with discretion.*

After managing your resources so that you will have enough to help those in need, you should actually help them. Take time to ask yourself the following questions and be very honest in your response. Wherever there is a shortcoming, you should work to make it better. Do you help your peers who are in need? Are you generally a helpful person? Do you assist those who you are able to? Do you lend to others when you are able to? Do you avoid offensive behavior? Do you keep confidential information confidential?

PRAYER: Lord help me be a good person - to lend and show favour. Please help me to guide my affairs with discretion in Jesus' name, Amen.

NOVEMBER 27

It's In My Heart

Psalm 119:11 (KJV)

> *Thy word have I hid in mine heart, that I might not sin against thee.*

Have you ever been in a situation where you were not sure of God's position on something? To know what God's position on anything is you have to read the Word, the Holy Bible. You also have to memorize the Bible so that you know what He says about different things. David actually hid the Word in his heart! If you memorize the Bible, whenever you meet upon a challenge you can pull out the scripture that speaks about it and allow that scripture to guide you, to help you in avoiding sin.

CHALLENGE: Memorize one scripture verse per day. At the end of the first year you will know 365 scriptures!

DAY 120

NOVEMBER 28

The Word: Illuminating Guide

Psalm 119:105 (KJV)

Thy word is a lamp unto my feet, and a light unto my path.

A lamp is a device used to give light, especially at night. It illuminates darkness. The Word of God also illuminates darkness allowing you to see where to put your feet. Let the Word of God guide your feet as you take each step along the path of life. Being at school, you should allow His Word to guide your interaction with your peers and with your teachers. At home you should also allow His Word to guide your interaction with your parents and siblings. Let God's Word guide you in everything you do.

PRAYER: Lord, I thank You for the guidance Your Word provides. In Jesus name I pray, amen.

DAY 121

NOVEMBER 29

God's Position is My Position

Psalm 119:165 (KJV)

> *Great peace have they which love thy law: and nothing shall offend them.*

Many people, even Christians, are offended by some scriptures in the Bible. The Bible is God's pure Word to us. God knows everything. He was before the beginning. He is sovereign. He does not lie. He is the greatest entity in the universe therefore whatever He said should be accepted by you, His child. Your acceptance of God's position on an issue should not depend on society's stance on the issue. Those who love God's law are not offended by them and they have peace knowing that His law is for their benefit.

DECLARATION: I have great peace. I love God's law. Nothing in the Word offends me.

NOVEMBER 30

Help from God

Psalm 121:1-2 (KJV)

> *I will lift up mine eyes unto the hills, from whence cometh my help.*
>
> *My help cometh from the LORD, which made heaven and earth.*

Are you in need of help right now? If you are not in need of help right now there will be a time in your life when you will be. Whenever you are faced with a problem take it to God. Jerusalem, the place where God dwelt, is on a hill so David looked to the hills for help. He was looking to God. Today the Holy Spirit is with you: (See John 14:26). He is a member of the Godhead. The Holy Spirit is your helper. He will interpret the things that Jesus has said for you. He will help you with whatever you need help with. Whenever you are in need of help ask Him to assist you.

DECLARATION: I will look to God for help. My help comes from God. I am assisted by the Holy Spirit.

DAY 123

DECEMBER 1

God the Builder

Psalm 127:1 (KJV)

> *Except the* Lord *build the house, they labour in vain that build it: except the* Lord *keep the city, the watchman waketh but in vain.*

Whatever you do independently of God is useless; it will not produce any lasting results. If you build a life without God it will crumble. Partner with God in planning your life. Let him be the Chief Architect of your life. Let God be the keeper of your life. He will keep you from immoral things, wandering and errors. Trust God with the building and protection of your life.

PRAYER: Father, help me to always involve You in whatever I do.

DAY 124

DECEMBER 2

He Puts What He Says Above Who He Is

Psalm 138:2 (KJV)

> *I will worship toward thy holy temple, and praise thy name for thy lovingkindness and for thy truth: for thou hast magnified thy word above all thy name.*

You can trust completely in God because He has glorified His Word above His name. If you go to Him and ask Him to do something He said He would do He will never say 'I can't do that today' or 'I won't be able to do that again'. He will perform His Word. Therefore, you can confidently apply every principle, carry out every instruction and be corrected and reprimanded by His Word knowing that your success is guaranteed. As such, even in the presence of great men, never be ashamed to praise God. Let them see your gratitude for all His goodness and faithfulness.

DECLARATION: God esteems His Word above His name. I confidently trust in Him. I will confidently apply every biblical principle and instruction. I will accept the correction and reprimand of God's Word.

DAY 125

DECEMBER 3

He Resolves Concerns

Psalm 138:8 (KJV)

> *The LORD will perfect that which concerneth me: thy mercy,*
> *O LORD, endureth for ever: forsake not the works of thine*
> *own hands.*

What are you concerned about? Whatever that concern is, God will take care of it. He will make it free of fault, He will perfect it. God will complete whatever He began in your life. Let this knowledge empower you to achieve extraordinary feats in school and in life. Go and do extraordinary things for God.

PRAYER: Lord, I thank You for perfecting the things that are of concern to me.

DAY 126

DECEMBER 4

He Thinks of Me

Psalm 139:17 (KJV)

> *How precious also are thy thoughts unto me, O God! how*
> *great is the sum of them!*

God thinks about you. It is amazing that God, the sovereign King should think about you. Think about it, does the leader of your country think about you, the individual? It is highly unlikely that he does, unless you are related to him/her. God thinks about you and His thoughts about you are precious. They are good thoughts. They are perfect. Today take some time to thank God for thinking about you. Ask God to help you to see yourself as He does.

DECLARATION: I think about myself as the Lord thinks about me. I see myself as the sum of God's thoughts towards me.

DECEMBER 5

Super Intelligent

Daniel 2: 19-23 (KJV)

> *Then was the secret revealed unto Daniel in a night vision.*
> *Then Daniel blessed the God of heaven.*

King Nebuchadnezzar had a dream which he could not remember and, when asked, some of his wise men did not know or could not interpret it. Because of this the king made a decree that all the wise men, including Daniel and his friends, should be killed. When Daniel heard about the decree he asked the king for time to consult God about the dream and its interpretation. Note that Daniel, a very intelligent man, did not ask for time to find out the details of the dream and its interpretation by his ability. Daniel teaches us that we should always acknowledge God and ask for His help and guidance in all that we do: (Read Dan. 2: 20-23).

PRAYER: Lord, today I ask You for wisdom, knowledge and understanding to be successful in studying. Please help me to be confident in Jesus name, amen.

DECEMBER 6

Divine Revelation

Daniel 2:27-30 (KJV)

> *Daniel answered in the presence of the king, and said, The secret which the king hath demanded cannot the wise men, the astrologers, the magicians, the soothsayers, shew unto the king;*
>
> *But there is a God in heaven that revealeth secrets, and maketh known to the king Nebuchadnezzar what shall be in the latter days. Thy dream, and the visions of thy head upon thy bed, are these;*

When Daniel appeared before the king with the revelation of the dream and its interpretation (see Dan. 2: 29 – 30) he did not take the glory for himself, instead he gave the glory to God. Do you give glory to God when you figure something out or when people praise your accomplishments? It is God who gives you wisdom therefore you should return all glory to Him.

PRAYER: Lord, please help me to acknowledge You in all that I do and all that I receive. When others praise me, let me point them to You who gave me talent and strength to accomplish great things, in Jesus name. Amen

DAY 129

DECEMBER 7

Loyalty in Friendship

Daniel 2:48-49 (KJV)

> *Then the king made Daniel a great man, and gave him many great gifts, and made him ruler over the whole province of Babylon, and chief of the governors over all the wise men of Babylon.*
>
> *Then Daniel requested of the king, and he set Shadrach, Meshach, and Abednego, over the affairs of the province of Babylon: but Daniel sat in the gate of the king.*

When Daniel asked God to reveal king Nebuchadnezzar's dream and its interpretation, his friends also joined him in prayer. When the king promoted him for accurately stating the dream and its interpretation, Daniel did not forget his friends who helped behind the scenes. In fact, he asked the king to promote them. Do you remember those who help you in private? How do you reward them? It is a kind, gracious and Godly thing to remember those who helped you along the way to success.

PRAYER: Lord, please help me to always remember and acknowledge those who help me in private.

DECEMBER 8

Stand For God

Daniel 3: 17-18 (KJV)

If it be so, our God whom we serve is able to deliver us from the burning fiery furnace, and he will deliver us out of thine hand, O king.

But if not, be it known unto thee, O king, that we will not serve thy gods, nor worship the golden image which thou hast set up.

Daniel and his friends made a habit of praying to God multiple times each day. One day king Nebuchadnezzar made a statue of himself and commanded that everyone bow down and worship it. The people were told that whoever disobeyed would be thrown into a fiery furnace. Even though Shadrach, Meshach, and Abednego knew the punishment for disobeying the king they said 'We will not bow and worship the statue. Our God has the ability to deliver us from the fiery furnace but if he doesn't we aren't going to worship the statue.' Today someone may not threaten to throw you in a fiery furnace if you refuse to commit idolatry however, you may be threatened with death. Do you have that kind of confidence in God that Shadrach, Meshach, and Abednego did? Would you take the same stance for God as they did?

PRAYER: Lord Jesus, grant me boldness to always stand for You. Please build my confidence in You so that no matter what circumstances, I will not bow to any other. Oh Lord, I will only bow to You my King, my Lord. Amen

DAY 131

DECEMBER 9

A Vibrant Prayer Life

Daniel 6:10 (KJV)

> *Now when Daniel knew that the writing was signed, he went into his house; and his windows being open in his chamber toward Jerusalem, he kneeled upon his knees three times a day, and prayed, and gave thanks before his God, as he did aforetime.*

Daniel knew that a scheme had been devised to entrap him. He was being persecuted because of his belief in and love for God which were displayed in his commitment to prayer. Yet, despite this Daniel continue praying to God as he normally would. Do you have a prayer life? If you do not have one you should start to develop one today. Like Daniel, there are people in other countries that face death if they pray. Remember them in your prayer.

PRAYER: Father, help me to always pray and not faint in Jesus name. Amen

DECEMBER 10

Do Not Be Enticed to Sin

Proverbs 1:10 (KJV)

My son, if sinners entice you, do not consent.

Today there is a lot of pressure to be part of the "in crowd". Most times the "in crowd" is not serving God or is serving Him half-heartedly. If you are attracted to or tempted by the fun to be had or the advantage of being friends with the "in crowd", remember that the wisest man advised you not to agree to be enticed by the activity or become part of the group. Make a decision for God by choosing Godly friends, people who will not tempt you by offering sinful pleasures.

DECLARATION: I will not be induced by the sinful enticement of men.

DECEMBER 11

Keep God's Commandments

Proverbs 3:1-2 (AMP)

> *My son, forget not my law or teaching, but let your heart keep my commandments;*
>
> *For length of days and years of a life [worth living] and tranquility [inward and outward and continuing through old age till death], these shall they add to you.*

God is very honest in His dealings. He tells you what to do and the reward for doing it. The great things about this is that there is no ambiguity on His part or your part. Proverbs 3:1 states two commandments for which there are three blessings: length of days, long life and tranquility or peace. The commands are (i) do not forget God's laws and (ii) let your heart keep God's commandments. It is only logical that you cannot forget what you do not know. The first command suggests that you know God's teachings. Do you? Commit to studying God's teachings so that you can get the blessing.

DECLARATION: Lord I will learn Your law or teaching. My heart will keep Your commandments and not forget them.

DECEMBER 12

Trust In God

Proverbs 3:5-6 (AMP)

> *Lean on, trust in, and be confident in the Lord with all*
> *your heart and mind and do not rely on your own insight or*
> *understanding.*
>
> *In all your ways know, recognize, and acknowledge Him,*
> *and He will direct and make straight and plain your paths.*

Sometimes we don't get it right: we look at all the factors and draw a conclusion that is completely wrong. Sometimes we conclude without having all the information. In such circumstances the conclusion is usually wrong. God knows everything. In whatever you do, accept the truth of His existence and recognize His importance. When you do this He will make your path plain and straight.

PRAYER: Lord, help me to lean on You, to trust and be confident in You with all my heart and mind. Help me not to rely on my own insight and understanding. Help me to always recognize You, knowing that You will direct my path.

DAY 135

DECEMBER 13

Self-elevation

Proverbs 3:7 (AMP)

> *Be not wise in your own eyes; reverently fear and worship the*
> *Lord and turn [entirely] away from evil.*

Humans have a tendency to develop inflated perceptions of themselves. This skewed perception often leads to self-ascribed wisdom. Self-wisdom leads to self-destruction. Therefore, do not be wise in your own eyes. Instead, develop a reverent fear of God and live your life in worship to Him. Make a decision to heed the advice of King Solomon.

DECLARATION: Father, I will turn from evil and seek You with reverent fear.

DECEMBER 14

Honour God With Your Money

Proverbs 3:9 (AMP)

> *Honor the Lord with your capital and sufficiency [from righteous labors] and with the firstfruits of all your income;*

You are to honour God with a portion of the money that you earn through honest means. You are also to honour Him with the first results/rewards of any undertaking or venture. When you do so, it shows your gratitude for His goodness. Economics teaches that the first profit is put back in the business to grow it however; natural principles never measure up to God's principles. His principles of prosperity have been tried, tested and proven. When you honour God with your first fruit, whether from work or from increase in your business, He will give you constant supply.

DECLARATION: I will honour God with my money. I will obey the principle of first fruit.

DECEMBER 15

Do Good

Proverbs 3:27 (AMP)

> *Withhold not good from those to whom it is due [its rightful owners], when it is in the power of your hand to do it.*

Doing good does good. It will help to protect you from diseases. It helps you to maintain good health generally. As long as you are capable of doing good to someone who is in need, do it. Do not say 'tomorrow I will assist you' when you can provide the assistance immediately. By practicing this principle you will also learn to be proactive, that is, to avoid procrastination.

DECLARATION: I will do good whenever I can. I will not put off doing good for another time when it is in my power to do it immediately.

DAY 138

DECEMBER 16

Pay Attention to The Word

Proverbs 4:20-22 (AMP)

> *My son, attend to my words; consent and submit to my sayings.*

> *Let them not depart from your sight; keep them in the center of your heart.*

> *For they are life to those who find them, healing and health to all their flesh.*

To attend to God's Word is to read it and meditate on it constantly. Do not read your Bible on Sundays only. It is important that you spend time reading the Bible by yourself and asking God questions. It is also important that you participate in Family Bible Hour. It is only through studying the Word that you will be able to know it and to grow spiritually. You will find life, healing and health in the Word.

PRAYER: O God, please give me grace to spend time reading Your Word. I want to have all that Your Word gives. In Jesus' name I pray, amen.

DAY 139

DECEMBER 17

Secret Ingredient – Wisdom

Proverbs 8:12 (AMP)

> *I, Wisdom [from God], make prudence my dwelling, and I find out knowledge and discretion.*

Do you believe that all things that are needed by human beings have been discovered? Even if you think so, I am pleased to tell you that there are still many things to be discovered. You will need experience, good judgment, understanding, insight, foresight and perception from God to make those discoveries. Study wisely and ask God to show you inner truths (insights) and provide you with the drive to succeed by applying good judgment.

CHALLENGE: Spend three sessions, of two minutes each, asking God for wisdom.

DAY 140

DECEMBER 18

Re-evaluate Friendships

Proverbs 9:6 (AMP)

> *Leave off, simple ones [forsake the foolish and simpleminded]*
> *and live! And walk in the way of insight and understanding.*

You may have some friends who hate the things of God. They make fun of the principles of the Bible. Some even encourage you to do things that are against what the Bible says, things that will result in your destruction. Explain who God is and the importance of your relationship with Him. Explain why you will not dishonor Him be doing the things they suggest. If they will not see your point, or if they refuse to respect your position, forsake them. Drop them. 'Defriend' them. 'Unfriend' them. If not, their pressure will increase and someday you will likely succumb. Preserve yourself. You have to do that if you are truly committed to God.

PRAYER: Lord, give me grace to forsake the foolish and walk in the way of insight and understanding.

DECEMBER 19

Care in Doing

Proverbs 10:4 (AMP)

> *He becomes poor who works with a slack and idle hand, but the hand of the diligent makes rich.*

Do not be dishonest in your interaction with others. Cheating hurts others and creates mistrust. Imagine a culture without integrity. Dishonesty leads to poverty. There are clear academic guidelines that govern cheating. One punishment for cheating is suspension or expulsion from school. Always be honest. Showing conscientiousness and care in your work will result in riches. Are the words in the assignment yours? Did you copy your classmate's work verbatim? Have you been proofreading your work? Is your work neat and tidy? Proofreading helps you to identify errors and a neat script will help your teacher to easily read your work. These things will likely result in you being awarded a higher grade so, take care in doing each task that you undertake.

DECLARATION: I take care to ensure that my work is of a high standard. I am diligent therefore the works of my hands will make me rich.

DAY 142

DECEMBER 20

Consider Your Legacy

Proverbs 13:22 (AMP)

> *A good man leaves an inheritance [of moral stability and goodness] to his children's children, and the wealth of the sinner [finds its way eventually] into the hands of the righteous, for whom it was laid up.*

If you grew up in church you would have heard the latter part of this verse. Have you ever heard the first part? Let's focus on it. You are God's child therefore you are good. As a good person you have a duty to leave an inheritance for your grandchildren. An inheritance does not only mean money. It also includes a legacy of praying, a Godly life and moral authority. This is an opportune time for you to begin to build a Godly, moral life. Start praying for your children and grandchildren. David prayed that the gold of Sheba would be given to Solomon and it was! (See Ps. 72:15) This season of learning is the time to lay a foundation so that you will be able to leave a financial inheritance for your grandchildren.

PRAYER: Lord, help me to be diligent. Teach me how to live so that generations after me may walk in Your ways, statues and commandments and never forsake Your law. In Jesus name, amen.

DAY 143

DECEMBER 21

Profit In Labour

Proverbs 14:23 (AMP)

In all labor there is profit, but idle talk leads only to poverty.

'If you can see it you can have it'. Many times students are told to visualize what they want to achieve and they will achieve it, but they are not told that they need to work in order to achieve what was visualized. Between visualization and accomplishment is WORK. *Visualize – WORK – Achieve.* No matter how many pictures you conjure in your brain, if you never lift a straw to make it happen it will never happen. If you want to become an accountant and imagine yourself being the best accountant but you never get qualified by learning the principles of accounting, you will never become an accountant much less the best accountant. At this stage of your life studying is your labour. In **all** labour there is profit, so work!

DECLARATION: I want to profit therefore I work. There is profit in all my work.

DAY 144

DECEMBER 22

Dedicate Your Works to God

Proverbs 16:3 (AMP)

> *Roll your works upon the Lord [commit and trust them wholly to Him; He will cause your thoughts to become agreeable to His will, and] so shall your plans be established and succeed.*

Have you ever wondered how you are going to accomplish your life goals? Do you want to become a scientist but Chemistry is getting more and more challenging? Partner with God. Roll your works upon Him. Give them completely over to Him and depend on Him completely. He will make your life goals become agreeable to His will. When you commit your works to God – give them totally to him - He will cause your plans to succeed.

PRAYER: Father God, I give all my works to You. I commit them to You. I know that You will allow my thoughts to all in line with Your will for me and so my plans will materialize and become successful.

DAY 145

DECEMBER 23

Love of Sleep Equals Poverty

Proverbs 20:13 (KJV)

> *Love not sleep, lest you come to poverty; open your eyes and you will be satisfied with bread.*

Doctors say eight to ten hours of sleep is enough for teenagers (14 – 17 years) while young adults (18 – 25 years) need 7 – 9 hours of sleep. However, we both know some persons who exceed their 'quota' daily. Some students get eleven or more hours of sleep each day! Why do people, especially students, sleep so much? The Lord warns that if you sleep too much you will become poor. Wake up, open your eyes. Get up and study (work) because in all labour there is profit. I learnt a memory gem while in primary (middle) school that you should memorize. It says, 'The heights by great men reached and kept were not attained by sudden flight, but they while their companions slept were toiling upwards through the night'.

DECLARATION: I will sleep for rest. I will not make sleep my past time. I will open my eyes and work because there is profit in work.

DECEMBER 24

Application

Proverbs 23:12 (AMP)

> *Apply your mind to instruction and correction and your ears*
> *to words of knowledge.*

Your teachers provide instruction in various subjects. Before you learnt to add you received instruction. As you did the addition exercises you were corrected along the way. When you followed the instructions methodically you got the correct answer. Now, for most of you, you have done addition so often that you do it without thinking of the instructions given to you by your teachers. The principles of adding are embedded in your mind. In the same way you should give your mind to the instructions and corrections of God. Carry them out until they become a part of you, until you do them without thinking.

PRAYER: Today I begin to apply my mind to instruction and correction. I begin to apply my ears to the Word of knowledge.

DAY 147

DECEMBER 25

Give to the Poor

Proverbs 28:27 (AMP)

> *He who gives to the poor will not want, but he who hides his*
> *eyes [from their want] will have many a curse.*

Is there a classmate or schoolmate who doesn't have as much resources as you do? Do you have enough to share with that person? Can you lend that person a pencil? Or, can you allow the person to copy the exercise from your text book? The principle here in Proverbs is that if you give to those who lack, you will not want. That is, God will take care of all your needs. He will provide for you. However, if you choose to ignore the needs of others, to look the other way, you will have many curses. Decide to develop a habit of sharing, especially with persons who are poor.

CHALLENGE: Develop the habit of sharing. Start today.

DECEMBER 26

Honouring Parents

Proverbs 30:17 (AMP)

> *The eye that mocketh at his father, and despiseth to obey his mother, the ravens of the valley shall pick it out, and the young eagles shall eat it.*

Throughout the Bible children are told to honour their parents. In Exodus 20:12, Deuteronomy 5:16, St. Mark 7:10 and Ephesians 6:2 children are commanded to honour their parents. The commandment to honour your parents is the first one with a promise attached to it: (See Ephesians 6:2). Those who dishonor their parents will die early. Some of you may say, 'But I'm going to die anyway'. If you just had that thought consider how you want to die – do you want the ravens of the valley to pick out your eyes? Hold your parents in high esteem. Regard them with great respect.

PRAYER: Lord, You commanded me to honour my parents. As of this day I will obey Your Word. Please help me to keep this promise in Jesus' name, amen.

DECEMBER 27

Lessons From the Ant

Proverbs 30:25 (AMP)

The ants are a people not strong, yet they lay up their food in the summer

The ants are physically weak but are shrewd in their behavior. They know that winter will come and during that time they will not be able to look for food. So, they prepare. To prepare for winter they store food in the summer months. What wisdom! What astuteness! What discipline! These are your summer years. Winter or adulthood is ahead, how will you take the time now to prepare for those years?

PRAYER: Lord, please enable me to prepare for adulthood. I want to live well in that season of life so please help me to make adequate preparation now.

DAY 150

DECEMBER 28

Lessons From the Coney

Proverbs 30:26 (KJV)

The conies are but a feeble folk, yet they make their houses in the rocks

Conies are small animals that look like rabbits. You will agree that they are not strong animals. Despite this the conies make their homes in the rocks. What? How do they get inside? They consistently chip away the rock until a space is created that can be used as their home. Some of you will learn about conies as agents of mechanical weathering in Geography class. The lesson from the coney is that no matter how large and overwhelming a task may appear to be, if you set small goals and work consistently at achieving them, eventually the large and seemingly overwhelming task will be accomplished.

CHALLENGE: Do large tasks by constantly doing the little things that are required to complete the entire task.

DECEMBER 29

Lessons from the Locust

Proverbs 30:27 (KJV)

The locusts have no king, yet they go forth all of them by bands

It is important to learn to work as a member of a team. In school, that skill is taught by placing you in groups. Group work is not the most loved way of completing an assignment but working as a team is a necessary skill that you need in order to succeed in the world. You are able to do more collectively than individually. A desert locust swarm can be 1,200 square kilometers in size and pack between 40 and 80 million locusts into less than one square kilometer. Each locust can eat its weight in plants each day, so a swarm of such size would eat about 423 million pounds of plants every day. As a result, a swarm of locusts can devastate crops and cause major agricultural damage leading to famine and starvation. The locusts are able to do this even though they do not have a leader. Do you see the value of team work?

DECLARATION: I value teamwork. I will learn how to work as a member of a team.

DAY 152

DECEMBER 30

Lessons from the Spider

Proverbs 30:28 (KJV)

> The spider taketh hold with her hands, and is in kings' palaces.

The spider makes silk which it uses to create a web and capture prey. Spiders are not exotic animals but they make their home in exotic places, including palaces. Where do you aspire to be in a few years? Are there different levels in the career or profession that you want to pursue? Despite the fact that your dream may seem unattainable, be like the spider – take hold of the dream and works towards it consistently. If you do, you will reach the highest level in your career or profession. Hang on in there.

DECLARATION: I will develop honest habits that will take me to the top of my profession.

DECEMBER 31

The Virtuous Woman

Proverbs 31:10 (KJV)

> *Who can find a virtuous woman? for her price is far above rubies.*

A virtuous woman is chaste. She has high moral standards. The question that is asked in Proverbs 31:10 suggests that she is not a dime a dozen, she is rare. Ladies, it is important that early in life you define the moral standards that you want to live by. It is important that those standards allow you to be described as virtuous. When you live by such standards you will be honouring God. Gentlemen, encourage young ladies along the way. Do not create traps for them to fall into. Ladies! Be morally and mentally strong. Be a virtuous woman.

DECLARATION:

Girls - I commit to being a virtuous woman

Boys - I commit to encouraging females to be virtuous as one day I want to marry a virtuous woman.

DAY 154

JANUARY 1

Seasons

Ecclesiastics 3:1 (KJV)

To everything there is a season, and a time to every purpose under the heaven

You know the four seasons – spring, summer, autumn and winter. In addition to these seasons of nature, there are seasons of life. This is the season in which you are to gain foundation knowledge by applying yourself to your studies. If you do not do what is required in this season, when the next season of life comes you will be at a disadvantage. You will have to 'play catch up' on what you failed to do in the previous season while trying to deal with the new one. Remember the ant? What would happen to ants if they refused to prepare for winter by storing food in summer and autumn? What will happen to you if you fail to do what is required of you in each season of your life?

PRAYER: Lord, help me to know the seasons of life and to do what is required in each season.

DAY 155

JANUARY 2

Give

Ecclesiastes 11:1 (KJV)

Cast thy bread upon the waters: for thou shalt find it after many days.

Giving to others is not first nature for a lot of persons. Humans tends to look out for themselves and then give whatever is left over. However, here King Solomon directs that we give liberally to the poor. Give whatever you have – money, time, resources, skills. This is very important as we will experience need at one point or another in life. The fact is that you do not know when you will need others to give to you. Giving today prepares you for tomorrow. It secures your future. This is because no matter how long it takes to come back to you, God or man will return it. So, today take an inventory of what you have to give and make a donation on the weekend.

CHALLENGE: Give to others.

DAY 156

JANUARY 3

At the End

Psalm 71:5 (KJV)

> *For thou art my hope, O Lord God: thou art my trust from*
> *my youth.*

God by His mercy, gave us grace to hope in Him! He is a sure hope. Your hope, when placed in Him, will not be misplaced. David was an adult when he wrote this Psalm. His testimony is that he had been hoping in God from he was a youth, much like you. As an older man he could reflect on his life with objectivity. This reflection led him to reaffirm and declare that God was his hope. Interestingly David declared that God was his hope from his youth. Like David, if you hope in God from your youth, you will have no regret in your adult years. Take the plunge. Hope in God. Put your trust in Him. Hope in God all the days of your life. When you become an adult you will join multiplied millions in saying that He has been your trust from your youth.

DECLARATION: At the end of my days I will say that God has been my trust from I was young.

JANUARY 4

Keep Away From Evil

I Thessalonians 5:22 (KJV)

Abstain from all appearance of evil.

Evil corrupts. It leads people down a path of pain and suffering. But, despite this many people embrace it. Have you ever been encouraged by your peers to do something that is wrong? Did you decline to do it? Or, did you think about the proposition and try to find several ways of justifying the wrong? The best response to an invitation to do evil is to decline, to restrain yourself from being a part of it. If you cannot stand your ground with a firm 'no', run. Keeping away from evil will preserve your destiny. It will preserve your life.

DECLARATION: I will abstain from evil. I will not participate in ungodly acts.

DAY 158

JANUARY 5

Never Obsolete

Isaiah 40:8 (KJV)

The grass withereth, the flower fadeth: but the word of our God shall stand for ever.

How beautiful are the flowers of the earth and the grass which blankets the ground. When watered by dew or rain they are most breathtaking however, they soon wither and die. God's Words are eternal. They will never die. Do you know of a second edition of the Bible? I thought that you didn't. I do not know of second edition either. God's Word has never been updated and it will never be. You can hope in God's Word because of this: 'The grass and flowers will fade but not God's Word'.

PRAYER: Lord, I thank You that Your Word will never change. I thank You that Your Word is forever!

DAY 159

JANUARY 6

No Debate

Psalm 119:89 (KJV)

For ever, O LORD, thy word is settled in heaven.

Mainstream media, social media, philosophers, influencers and social commentator bombard your space to tell you what to believe about moral, religious, social and political matters. It is as if everyone is competing to define your position on these matters. Some even advocate that the Bible is not relevant to modern issues however, God's Words are final. They are settled in heaven. Let the Word of God guide you in taking a position on moral, religious, social and political matters. Let it guide your outlook in all areas of life.

DECLARATION: The Bible, God's Word is my source of information about what is right and true. It is my compass in life.

DAY 160

JANUARY 7

Sexual Purity

Song of Solomon 2:7 (KJV)

> *I charge you, O ye daughters of Jerusalem, by the roes, and by the hinds of the field, that ye stir not up, nor awake my love, till he please.*

The changes that you are experiencing in your teenage years are not unique to you. In fact, every young man/woman has experienced them since the beginning of time. As the body of a teenager changes he/she begins to like members of the opposite sex. This young woman in the scripture provides a model way of dealing with such changes and emotions. She liked a young man and her friends tried to encourage her to pursue it. She knew where those feelings could lead so she asked them not to stir up or excite them. You too should do the same at this stage of your life. Ask your friend not to stir up your love for or interest in a member of the opposite sex.

PRAYER: Lord, give me grace to remain pure before You.

DAY 161

JANUARY 8

Isaiah 36:22 (KJV)

> *Then came Eliakim, the son of Hilkiah, that was over the household, and Shebna the scribe, and Joah, the son of Asaph, the recorder, to Hezekiah with their clothes rent, and told him the words of Rabshakeh.*

Isaiah 37:1 (KJV)

> *And it came to pass, when king Hezekiah heard it, that he rent his clothes, and covered himself with sackcloth, and went into the house of the LORD.*

The king of Assyria went to fight against king Hezekiah. One of the lieutenants of the king of Assyria delivered a message to king Hezekiah's scribe and recorder. The message was designed to drive fear in king Hezekiah. When he heard the message king Hezekiah immediately went to God. Sometimes when discouraging situations arise the first thing we do is to call a friend. We discuss it for days and sometimes weeks. It is important to note that king Hezekiah did not call the elders when he got the message. He did not discuss it with anyone. He simply went to the Lord with it. When faced with discouragement do as king Hezekiah did, go to God first.

DECLARATION: God is my first resort. I will not try other things before going to Him. He is the person to whom I go first.

JANUARY 9

Put It Before God

Isaiah 37:14 (KJV)

And Hezekiah received the letter from the hand of the messengers, and read it: and Hezekiah went up unto the house of the LORD, and spread it before the LORD.

When the king of Assyria did not succeed in intimidating king Hezekiah on the first attempt he sent another message. This time the message was written in a letter. There was no likelihood that it would be relayed incorrectly or that king Hezekiah would interpret it incorrectly. When king Hezekiah read the letter he immediately took it to the house of God, spread it out and prayed. Sometimes problems are persistent and present themselves in different forms. Whatever forms it comes in, model king Hezekiah. Place it before the Lord. Do you or someone that you know need to do this?

CHALLENGE: Remember the story of king Hezekiah for the day you will need it and also share it with someone who needs it today.

JANUARY 10

Your Works Create Favour

Isaiah 38:5 (KJV)

> *Go, and say to Hezekiah, Thus saith the LORD, the God of David thy father, I have heard thy prayer, I have seen thy tears: behold, I will add unto thy days fifteen years.*

The Lord sent Isaiah the prophet to tell king Hezekiah that he should prepare his affairs because he was going to die shortly: (See Isaiah 38:1-2). King Hezekiah had a history of going to God in times of distress and this time, when his life was at stake, it was no different. Upon receiving the message the king turned on his bed and prayed, "Remember now, O LORD, I beseech thee, how I have walked before thee in truth and with a perfect heart, and have done that which is good in thy sight": (Isaiah 30:3 KJV). O what a blessedness to know that God hears and answers prayer. If king Hezekiah had not walked uprightly before God, in obedience to His commandments, he could not have made the claims that he did. When you need to go to God in prayer to request mercy, will your claim be true? Only you can determine that.

PRAYER: Lord, please help me to have a perfect heart and to walk uprightly before You.

JANUARY 11

Speak Well of Your Successor

Deuteronomy 31:7 (KJV)

> *And Moses called unto Joshua, and said unto him in the sight of all Israel, Be strong and of a good courage: for thou must go with this people unto the land which the LORD hath sworn unto their fathers to give them; and thou shalt cause them to inherit it.*

Moses was the leader of the children of Israel. He successfully led them out of bondage in Egypt. Joshua was Moses' helper. He served Moses faithfully. When Moses died he would become the leader of the children of Israel. In preparation for Joshua's leadership, just before his death Moses affirmed him in front of everyone. He called Joshua before the children of Israel and encouraged him. When you are leaving a position of leadership make way for your successor. Speak well of him or her. Make him or her look good in the eyes of those he or she will lead. When people know that you have confidence in your successor they will follow his or her leadership without resistance.

DECLARATION: I will speak well of my successors.

JANUARY 12

Speak Well of Your Predecessor

Joshua 22:5 (KJV)

> *But take diligent heed to do the commandment and the law,*
> *which Moses the servant of the LORD charged you, to love the*
> *LORD your God, and to walk in all his ways, and to keep his*
> *commandments, and to cleave unto him, and to serve him*
> *with all your heart and with all your soul.*

Joshua succeeded Moses as leader of Israel. When he became leader he could have decided to publish all that Moses did that he was not in agreement with. He could have broadcasted all of Moses' shortcomings and failures. It could have been the time when he decided to pursue his own agenda but he obeyed God's command to follow what Moses modelled. When you succeed someone in leadership do not seek to tear them down. Do not discontinue the good things that they put in place instead, continue to build upon them and if you are not able to take that decision, at least recommend that they be continued.

DECLARATION: I will speak well of my predecessor.

JANUARY 13

Strength

Isaiah 40:29 (KJV)

> *He giveth power to the faint; and to them that have no might he increaseth strength.*

Feeling weary? Tell God. He has strength for himself and for you. His power is inexhaustible. He has limitless strength. God has always ministered strength to His people who are weak and down trodden. This is no different. Even if you are on your last breath, reach out to Him because He will strengthen you. That includes giving you physical strength and strengthening your faith. He will give you power. He will give you strength. You will be made strong in Him.

PRAYER: Thank you Lord for increasing my strength when I faint. Thank You for being faithful in keeping Your promises. Amen.

DAY 167

JANUARY 14

Renewed Strength

Isaiah 40: 30-31 (KJV)

> *Even the youths shall faint and be weary, and the young men shall utterly fall:*
>
> *But they that wait upon the LORD shall renew their strength; they shall mount up with wings as eagles; they shall run, and not be weary; and they shall walk, and not faint.*

Young people often think that they are strong boundless people. However, if you are true to yourself you will admit that you get weak from time to time, even for extended periods. You have struggles that cause you to feel faint. Despite the fact that you get tired under the strains and stresses of life, this does not have to be your constant reality. You are guaranteed renewal if you wait on God.

PRAYER: Teach me to wait on You Lord so that I will benefit from renewed strength; not being weary, not fainting but having ways to soar like the eagle through storms and over mountains, being able to ascend to high altitude and being perceptive to earn great rewards.

CHALLENGE: Identify the four advantages of waiting on God.

DAY 168

JANUARY 15

Assurance in Trouble

Isaiah 43:2 (KJV)

> *When thou passest through the waters, I will be with thee;*
> *and through the rivers, they shall not overflow thee: when*
> *thou walkest through the fire, thou shalt not be burned;*
> *neither shall the flame kindle upon thee.*

Life can seem overwhelming. Water overwhelms and fire consumes. No matter what the calamity – a body of water, a flowing river or fire - despite the intensity of it, always remember that God will preserve you. He promised to be with you and because He will be there you will be ok. You will not drown (See Joshua 3) and you will not be consumed (See Daniel 3:25, 27). You will survive to encourage someone else. You will be alright.

PRAYER: Father God, I thank You for the assurance that You will be with me in difficult time in Jesus name, amen.

DAY 169

JANUARY 16

Reason with God

Isaiah 43:26 (KJV)

> *Put me in remembrance: let us plead together: declare thou,*
> *that thou mayest be justified.*

God invited Israel to remind Him of their merits, their good deeds. He told them to argue the points that were in favour of their acquittal from the charge of guilt. Do not hold on to guilt. You can remind God of His promises so that by His grace you may be acquitted from any charge of guilt. If you have done wrong, seek forgiveness by the blood of Jesus and in the name of Jesus. If you are believing for something, remind God of His Word. Reason with Him.

PRAYER: Lord, help me to know Your Word so that I can have discussions about it with You.

JANUARY 17

Incomparable

Isaiah 46:5 (KJV)

> *To whom will ye liken me, and make me equal, and compare me, that we may be like?*

Sometime during youth many persons find themselves questioning the sovereignty of God. Here God was saying to Israel, 'If you are tempted to do that, seriously consider if you can find another god, who can be compared to Me'. No one can be compared to God. Everything and everyone pales in comparison to Him. He is in a category by Himself. He is God, not to be likened to any other god. He is superior to all. Genesis 1 records what He has done. No one can claim to have created anything similar. God's testimony is greater than anyone else's (See 1 John 5:9). In Isaiah 45:5 He said that He is God and there is none greater than He is. His authority is absolute. He is sovereign.

CONFESSION: Lord, You are God. There is none like You. There is none that is equal to You. There is none that can be compared to You.

DAY 171

JANUARY 18

Price Paid

Isaiah 53:5 (KJV)

But he was wounded for our transgressions, he was bruised for our iniquities: the chastisement of our peace was upon him; and with his stripes we are healed.

The prophet Isaiah foretold the death of Jesus and the gift of salvation that was made possible by His resurrection. In foretelling the death of Jesus he also told us of the benefits all humans would receive because of His death. At Calvary Jesus was beaten and wounded. All of this was to enable us to have salvation, peace, joy, prosperity and healing. Do you want to experience salvation, peace and healing? Put your trust in Jesus. Give him your heart, body and soul. Surrender your all to Him. Accept the gift of salvation today and experience all that it brings.

PRAYER: Jesus, thank You for going to the cross for me. Today I surrender to You. Be my Lord. In Your name I pray, amen.

JANUARY 19

Endure

St. Matthew 27:46 (KJV)

> *And about the ninth hour Jesus cried with a loud voice, saying, Eli, Eli, lama sabachthani? that is to say, My God, my God, why hast thou forsaken me?*

Oftentimes people give up midway through a project or a phase of life. Jesus felt lonely while He was on the cross but He endured and died because that was His purpose for coming to the earth. Will you endure and accomplish your purpose in school? Will you complete the task you were given even though you get lonely sometimes? No matter how lonely you feel, God is always with you. Endure the process. Today we enjoy salvation because Jesus endured. Think about the many lives that will be changed because you endured.

PRAYER: Lord Jesus help me to remember that I am never alone and You are always with me even as Your Father was with You while You endured the cross for me. Amen

JANUARY 20

Right Time

Isaiah 55:6 (KJV)

> *Seek ye the LORD while he may be found, call ye upon him*
> *while he is near*

'Seek' means to look for something purposefully, intently. God wants you to look for Him with intent, not casually or in passing. He wants you to seek Him while grace is available, before "too late" becomes a reality. One great way of seeking God is to spend purposeful time searching the scriptures to know who He is. This search will develop discipline in you. You can apply the discipline that you developed in seeking God to seeking the answers to questions for your projects and assignments. Preserve that discipline all the days of your life.

CONFESSION: I will seek the Lord.

JANUARY 21

Holy Spirit: Aid Worker

Isaiah 59:19b (KJV)

> *When the enemy shall come in like a flood, the Spirit of the*
> *LORD shall lift up a standard against him.*

In life there are different battles that you will have to fight. If, during a battle, you every feel as if you are drowning, if you feel the waters rising above your head just call to the Lord. "Help!" is a sufficient cry. When you call, the Holy Spirit will come to your assistance. He will stem the rising tide of the enemy.

PRAYER: Lord, I thank You that the Holy Spirit is my ally and He will always come to my assistance.

JANUARY 22

Strong In God

Ephesians 6:10-12 (KJV)

> *Finally, my brethren, be strong in the Lord, and in the power of his might.*
>
> *Put on the whole armour of God, that ye may be able to stand against the wiles of the devil.*

When others do mean things to us we see it as them doing it, of them being cruel and uncaring. But according to Ephesians 6:12 we are not fighting against flesh and blood that is, human beings. Instead, you are fighting against the celestial hierarchy of the demonic world, and spiritual wickedness in high places. Sometimes when people do us wrong we retaliate against the person. However, most of the mean things that others do to you are motivated by evil spirits and it is against those spirits that you must fight. Do not retaliate by praying for their demise. Instead, do as Prophet Michael Carter instructs, "Pray for the spirit in them to be fired".

DECLARATION: I will not allow the devil to use me.

JANUARY 23

The Armour

Ephesians 6:13 (KJV)

> *Wherefore take unto you the whole armour of God, that ye may be able to withstand in the evil day, and having done all, to stand.*

To win the battle against principalities, powers, the rulers of the darkness of this world, and spiritual wickedness in high places you must dress appropriately. Each day you must put on the garments outlined in Ephesians 6:14-17. Starting today, be sure to memorize each part of the armour and put them on every morning during your prayer time.

PRAYER: Father God, I thank You for my salvation. Please keep my mind and eyes focused on You. Lord, let me see things as You do. I put on the breastplate of righteousness. I am Your righteousness in Christ Jesus and I am protected from all condemnation. I put on the belt of truth. I will live a life of honesty and integrity. Show me Your truth O God. I put on the shoes of the gospel of peace. Lord, help me to always be ready to share the gospel. I take the shield of faith and use it against every lie Satan tells. I take the sword of the Spirit, Your Word and use it to protect myself and my family from Satan and all his followers. Lord, I will pray throughout this day. My spirit will communicate with the Holy Spirit in all prayer throughout the day, in Jesus name. Amen

JANUARY 24

Guided By God

Jeremiah 10:23 (KJV)

O Lord, I know that the way of man is not in himself: it is not in man that walketh to direct his steps.

Sometimes we think that we are in absolute control of our lives but that is not so. The way your life goes will depend on more than personal choice; it will be determined by divine providence. Many prayers were prayed over you long before you were born. Your parents may have even covenanted with the Lord. Look out for and allow His divine providence to guide you. Be obedient to the direction in which God leads you. He is leading you to live a purpose accomplished life.

DECLARATION: I submit to God and allow Him to direct my steps.

DAY 178

JANUARY 25

Illuminated Path

Psalm 119:105 (KJV)

Thy word is a lamp unto my feet, and a light unto my path.

God's Word provides guidance along the path of life. It lights the way, showing you where to go. It shows you what to avoid. It gives guidance about your attitude, conduct, choices and aspirations. It will provide direction in doubt. It will direct you in dark and difficult times. It is amazing that God does this for us. With this guide in hand, make sure to use it. Do not be like many who ignore the Word and suffer the roadblocks and setbacks of life because of ignorance. A GPS system will make the journey smoother. Be guided by the Word. Use it to guide you along the journey of life.

PRAYER: Lord, I thank You for giving Your Word which shows where I am to go along the path of life.

DAY 179

JANUARY 26

Anointed For Excellence

Exodus 31:3 (KJV)

> *And I have filled him with the spirit of God, in wisdom, and in understanding, and in knowledge, and in all manner of workmanship,*

God told Moses to make the tabernacle and He gave him the dimensions of it. God then anointed men to do the work of building His dwelling place. Here God was, pouring wisdom, knowledge and understanding into men. You are or will soon be at the stage of choosing the subjects/courses that will qualify you for your career. You need the wisdom of God to choose and to excel in your chosen field. Ask God to guide you in your choice. The Holy Spirit is with you. He is the Spirit of wisdom, knowledge and understanding. He will teach you all thing. He will cause you to remember all things. He is crying in the streets, desiring a place to lodge, invite him into your life. May you be filled with the spirit of excellence.

PRAYER: O Lord, please guide me as I make career decisions. Holy Spirit I invite you to dwell in my life forever. Lord, please put the Spirit of wisdom, understanding, knowledge and excellence upon me so that I excel for Your glory. In Jesus name, amen.

DAY 180

JANUARY 27

Eat the Word

Jeremiah 15:16 (KJV)

> *Thy words were found, and I did eat them; and thy word was unto me the joy and rejoicing of mine heart: for I am called by thy name, O LORD God of hosts*

When the prophet was given God's revealed Word he received it with joy. He gladly consumed it. You have the Bible which is God's Word. Receive it with gladness, internalize it for sustenance. There are still people groups who do not have the written Word. You are in a very privileged position. You own the Word, you have a Bible. Use it effectively. The prophet also said that he was called by the name of God. This means that he was consecrated to God – he was made sacred and dedicated to the service of God. A consecrated life is sustained by a diet of the Word. Eat the Word.

PRAYER: Pray for grace to feed on the Word daily. Pray that people groups that do not have the Bible translated in their language will get it soon. Pray also for the wisdom of Bible translators.

DAY 181

JANUARY 28

Jeremiah 17:7 (KJV)

Blessed is the man that trusteth in the LORD, and whose hope the LORD is.

There is a blessing that is received when a person trusts and hopes in God. Jeremiah 17:8 tells us that the person who trusts in God is like a tree that always has water. Water is an essential ingredient for plant and human growth. This tree that Jeremiah speaks of has an abundant supply of water because of where it was planted – by the stream. The tree is like the child of God. That person has constant supply of water and space to grow unrestrictedly. He or she is an evergreen. The heat of the day does not affect his or her produce. He or she is always producing, even in times of scarcity. Where have you placed your trust? Where have you placed your hope? If your trust and your hope are not in God, today is the day to change that.

DECLARATION: Lord, I trust in You. I place my hope in You.

DAY 182

JANUARY 29

No Easy Walk

Jeremiah 20:7-10 (KJV)

> *O LORD, thou hast deceived me, and I was deceived; thou art stronger than I, and hast prevailed: I am in derision daily, every one mocketh me.*

Jeremiah was called by God to be a prophet however; he was beaten, mocked and imprisoned: (See Jeremiah 20:8-10). God did not tell him that these things would have happened so he complained. We are no different from Jeremiah. We start doing what God called us to do and, when challenges arise, we complain to Him. Your walk with Jesus will not be easy. You may be mocked by your peers but endure the shame because one day God will reward you for the sincere work that you do for Him. Stay the course and fulfill your purpose.

PRAYER: Father, please give me grace to accept all that it means to be Your child.

JANUARY 30

Permanent Covenant

Jeremiah 33:19-21 (KJV)

> *Thus says the Lord: 'If you can break My covenant with the day and My covenant with the night, so that there will not be day and night in their season,*
>
> *then My covenant may also be broken with David My servant, so that he shall not have a son to reign on his throne, and with the Levites, the priests, My ministers.*

The Bible contains God's covenants with us. A covenant is binding agreement between God and His people. Today the courts of law are full of cases in which parties sue each other for breaching a contract or an agreement. God will not breach His covenant with us and no third party can. In fact, God said the only way His covenant with David could be broken is if it was possible to break His covenant with the day and the night. It is impossible for anyone to cause night and day to not appear. Therefore, God's covenants cannot be broken. What an assurance! His covenant with You is for a thousand generations. Hallelujah!

PRAYER: Lord, I thank You that You cannot break Your covenants. I thank You for the integrity with which You entered those covenants. I will do my part to have Your covenants fulfilled in my life, in Jesus name. Amen

DAY 184

JANUARY 31

Silence

Lamentations 3:26 (KJV)

> *It is good that a man should both hope and quietly wait for the salvation of the LORD.*

Sometimes you want things now, without any wait period. However, the prophet says it is good for you to hope and *quietly wait* for God. In this time of quiet waiting you can strengthen your relationship with God. During your time of *quiet wait* God will preserve you from ruin, harm and loss. Can you think of any other benefits of hoping and quietly waiting for the Lord? List the benefits of (a) hoping in God and (b) quietly waiting on God.

DECLARATION: I will hope in God. I will quietly wait for the salvation of the Lord.

DAY 185

FEBRUARY 1

Say What God Says

Ezekiel 37:3a (KJV)

Again he said unto me, Prophesy upon these bones

In Ezekiel 37:1-10 God questions the prophet as to whether dry bones could live again! Like you and I would, the prophet gave the politically correct answer, 'Lord, you know'. At first blush the answer seems barefaced but in his response he acknowledged that God is all-knowing. The Lord took no offence and instructed Ezekiel what to say to the bones. When he obeyed the skeletons began to take on life sustaining character: flesh grew, blood flowed through veins and they began to breathe. Incredible! The Bible is God's Word to you. Can you imagine what will happen when you obey what He is saying to you?

DECLARATION: As I prophesy God's Word over my life I will take on life sustaining character. I will live and do valiantly for Him. With God's direction I will prophesy to dead situations in my life and they will live.

DAY 186

FEBRUARY 2

Honour Through Obedience

Daniel 1:8a (KJV)

> *But Daniel purposed in his heart that he would not defile himself with the portion of the king's meat, nor with the wine which he drank*

Daniel and his friends were captured and taken from Israel to Babylon. They were chosen to attend a special school and to eat the same food as the king ate. Can you imagine how mouthwatering the food was? No doubt many felt honoured to be chosen like that but not Daniel and his friends. They refused to eat the same food as the king because they knew that if they did they would be breaking the laws that God gave to Moses in the book of Leviticus. Who would know if they ate it? It could have been their secret but Daniel and his friends honoured God through their integrity and obedience. You will be faced with many choices. Be sure to do what is right, even when no one is watching.

PRAYER: Lord please help me to obey Your Word and do the things that are right, even when my parents are not around. Help me Lord to stay true to You and Your Word always, in Jesus' name. Amen

FEBRUARY 3

Elevated by Obedience

Daniel 1:20 (KJV)

> *And in all matters of wisdom and understanding, that the*
> *king enquired of them, he found them ten times better than*
> *all the magicians and astrologers that were in all his realm.*

After abstaining from the king's food, Daniel and his friends were examined and found to be fairer and fatter than their peers who ate the king's food. They were also found to be more knowledgeable. This depth and breadth of knowledge and skill in learning and wisdom had been given to them by God whom they honoured. If you honour God you will see His blessings in your life just as Daniel and his friends did.

DECLARATION: I will stay true to God's Word because in doing so I will be wiser and stronger, full of knowledge and understanding to accomplish great things.

FEBRUARY 4

Knowledge for Change

Hosea 4:6 (KJV)

> *My people are destroyed for lack of knowledge: because thou*
> *hast rejected knowledge, I will also reject thee, that thou shalt*
> *be no priest to me: seeing thou hast forgotten the law of thy*
> *God, I will also forget thy children.*

If you do not know God and His ways you will make wrong choices. Even today, the people of God continually experience destruction because they lack knowledge. It is strongly advisable that you get to know God. Knowing God will take time but you should invest in the greatest relationship you will ever have and ever need. Do not reject God as He will reject you and the generations after you. Set the right precedent and chart a God-directed course for you, your family and the generations after you. Be the change.

PRAYER: Lord please help me to love knowledge and to pursue it.

DAY 189

FEBRUARY 5

God's Requirements

Micah 6:8 (KJV)

> *He hath shewed thee, O man, what is good; and what doth*
> *the LORD require of thee, but to do justly, and to love mercy,*
> *and to walk humbly with thy God?*

God requires you to be and do justly in every interaction with others. To do justly means that you will not cheat on exams, that you will do your homework by yourself and not have your cousin do it for you. He also requires you to show mercy and be humble. To show mercy means that you will forgive persons who have wronged you. You will not require the pound of flesh. Humility means being modest about your importance. Do not beat your chest and say, "Do you know who I am?"

PRAYER: Lord help me to do justice, to love kindness and mercy, to humble myself and to walk humbly before You.

FEBRUARY 6

Write the Vision

Habakkuk 2:2 (KJV)

And the LORD answered me, and said, Write the vision, and make it plain upon tables, that he may run that readeth it.

Sometimes when you decide to do something you create a mental picture of it and you are excited for a while. Soon the picture begins to fade and the excitement begins to ebb. When you write your dreams and visions it prevents that from happening. Each time you read what you wrote, the excitement will be rekindled. The picture will become sharper. Write your dreams, visions and aspirations. Work them. Re-visit them from time to time and you will be amazed at what you have accomplished. You will also be shocked at the fuel you get from re-visiting them.

DECLARATION: I will write the vision. Each time I read the vision I will be re-energized.

DAY 191

FEBRUARY 7

Retaliation

St. Matthew 5:38-39 (KJV)

Ye have heard that it hath been said, An eye for an eye, and a tooth for a tooth:

But I say unto you, That ye resist not evil: but whosoever shall smite thee on thy right cheek, turn to him the other also.

When someone causes you hurt the natural response is to retaliate by doing the same thing or worse to them. However, retaliation can cause the situation to escalate. Instead of retaliating, turn the other cheek. Do whatever is necessary to diffuse the situation. By doing so you may preserve your life.

CHALLENGE: Learn to turn the other cheek. (This means that you will have to practice!)

DAY 192

FEBRUARY 8

The Model Prayer

St. Matthew 6:9 (KJV)

> *But thou, when thou prayest, enter into thy closet, and when thou hast shut thy door, pray to thy Father which is in secret; and thy Father which seeth in secret shall reward thee openly.*

Prayer is the means by which we communicate with God but people often say they do not know how to pray. If you feel that way, practice praying the prayer that Jesus taught His disciples to pray. Prayer takes practice. The Holy Spirit will teach you how to pray. I believe that every Christian should develop the discipline of prayer. There are many realms in prayer that you can go to. Realms that will enable you to positively affect your community, nation or region. God acts upon the prayers of His people. Get on your knees in a private place and begin to pray. You will usher in revival and the coming of our Lord Jesus Christ.

CHALLENGE: Practice prayer. Look at your watch. Time yourself. Pray for 10 minutes.

FEBRUARY 9

He Provides I

St. Matthew 6:25 (KJV)

> *Therefore I say unto you, Take no thought for your life, what ye shall eat, or what ye shall drink; nor yet for your body, what ye shall put on. Is not the life more than meat, and the body than raiment?*

What are you concerned about? How your tuition will be paid? What you will eat? Whether you will make it through high school? Whether you will be able to afford the college of your choice? Whatever it is, be assured that God will provide. Every day He faithfully provides for the flowers and the birds. He will provide for you. Have unwavering faith and believe that He will come through for you.

DECLARATION: God is my Provider.

DAY 194

FEBRUARY 10

He Provides II

St. Matthew 6:31-34 (KJV)

> *Therefore take no thought, saying, What shall we eat? or,*
> *What shall we drink? or, Wherewithal shall we be clothed?*

Do you know of at least one child who, because of financial difficulties, attend school without eating breakfast and is not able to afford lunch. At the end of the day that child may even return home to no food. If you know someone in this situation, will you share your lunch with him or her? Will you refer that person to the Guidance Counsellor? If you are in this situation ask God to provide for you. Speak to your Guidance Counsellor or Pastor who may be able to provide assistance.

CHALLENGE: Be God's hands of provision.

DAY 195

FEBRUARY 11

Ask, Seek, Knock

St. Matthew 7:7-8 (KJV)

Ask, and it shall be given you; seek, and ye shall find; knock,
and it shall be opened unto you:

For every one that asketh receiveth; and he that seeketh
findeth; and to him that knocketh it shall be opened.

When you pray for something you are making a request of God. There
are different levels of intensity in making that request. To ASK is simply
to articulate, in the form of a request, what you want another person to do
or to give. To SEEK is to make a request of someone with a greater level
of intensity than asking. It is an attempt to find something with diligence
and intensity. When you KNOCK you strike a surface noisily with the
intention of attracting a person's attention. Keep asking, keep seeking, and
keep knocking. When you ask you will receive. When you seek you will
find. When you knock the door will be opened.

DECLARATION: I will ask. I will seek. I will knock.

DAY 196

FEBRUARY 12

Kingdom Labourer

St. Matthew 9:36-38 (KJV)

> *But when he saw the multitudes, he was moved with compassion on them, because they fainted, and were scattered abroad, as sheep having no shepherd.*
>
> *Then saith he unto his disciples, The harvest truly is plenteous, but the labourers are few;*
>
> *Pray ye therefore the Lord of the harvest, that he will send forth labourers into his harvest.*

Jesus looked at the people gathered and it appeared that they had no one to lead them. People are open to the gospel of Jesus. They are willing to hear. Are all the students at your school saved? Can you imagine what your school environment and the society would be like if everyone was saved? Your school is a field where the harvest is plenteous – there are many persons whose hearts are ready to hear the gospel. Will you be a labourer in your school, someone who introduces others to Jesus? Pray that God equips you with boldness to share the gospel message with those in your school.

PRAYER: O God, grace to be a labourer working to spread the gospel of Jesus Christ.

DAY 197

FEBRUARY 13

Mustard Seed Faith

St. Matthew 17:20 (KJV)

> *And Jesus said unto them, Because of your unbelief: for verily*
> *I say unto you, If ye have faith as a grain of mustard seed, ye*
> *shall say unto this mountain, Remove hence to yonder place;*
> *and it shall remove; and nothing shall be impossible unto you.*

Faith is a creative force that defies natural laws. Look at a mustard seed. See how small it is? Look at a mountain. See how large it is? Jesus said that faith the size of a mustard seed, in the absence of doubt, can remove a mountain. Every child of God was given the measure of faith: (See Romans 12:3). This means that if you use the faith you have, no matter how small it is, nothing will be impossible to you.

DECLARATION: I will use my faith.

DAY 198

FEBRUARY 14

Unlimited Forgiveness

St. Matthew 18:21-22 (KJV)

> *Then came Peter to him, and said, Lord, how oft shall my brother sin against me, and I forgive him? till seven times?*
>
> *Jesus saith unto him, I say not unto thee, Until seven times: but, Until seventy times seven.*

Based on Jesus' response to Peter you are to forgive each person 490 times. Do not get too excited just yet. Put away the Forgiveness Record Book. Imagine keeping a record of all the times you forgive everyone who offends you. You would not have enough books to keep record and if you did, you would have to become a Forgiveness Clerk by profession. Keeping record of how many times you forgave each person could be a full-time job. I believe that Jesus was saying to Peter, 'Forgive freely'. Forgive as many times as is needed. It is for your benefit.

PRAYER: Father God, please enable me with grace to give unlimited forgiveness to those who wrong me.

FEBRUARY 15

Go!

St. Matthew 28:19-20 (KJV)

> *Go ye therefore, and teach all nations, baptizing them in the name of the Father, and of the Son, and of the Holy Ghost:*
>
> *Teaching them to observe all things whatsoever I have commanded you: and, lo, I am with you always, even unto the end of the world. Amen*

This was Jesus' last instruction to all His followers. It is called the Great Commission. This commission should be taken literally. Every follower of Christ should share the gospel. Go and share the gospel. You may not be able to go to a foreign country but you live in a community, a parish, a county, a state, a country. You are a student at a school and you are a member of at least one club or other social organization. Share the gospel with people you encounter. Give financially to those who go overseas to share the gospel.

DECLARATION: I will work to spread of the gospel throughout the world.

FEBRUARY 16

Good from Bad

Genesis 45:5 (KJV)

> *Now therefore be not grieved, nor angry with yourselves, that ye sold me hither: for God did send me before you to preserve life.*

Sometimes when bad things happen all you can see in that moment is the bad thing. Most times you cannot see beyond it. However, no matter how bad the situation is, something positive will come out of it. I therefore encourage you to look for the positive in every situation. Joseph could have allowed hatred to develop in his heart toward his brothers. He did not do that, he looked for the positive and acknowledged it. Will you look for the good thing that can come from an adverse situation?

DECLARATION: I will identify the good or potential good in every adverse situation. I refuse to be bitter or resentful.

FEBRUARY 17

Guaranteed Reward

St. Mark 9:41 (KJV)

> *For whosoever shall give you a cup of water to drink in my name, because ye belong to Christ, verily I say unto you, he shall not lose his reward.*

When you show kindness to those who are members of the body of Christ you will received a sure reward. Even if your act of kindness is giving a cup of water to a child of God, you will received the reward for it. The act of kindness that is recorded in Mark is one of the smallest acts of kindness that anyone can do. It is also one of the lowest threshold of respect, of acknowledgment of a person's humanity. As a child of God you are guaranteed a reward for your humblest and lowliest act to a member of the body of Jesus Christ.

DECLARATION: For the rest of my life I will do good to people, especially to those in the body of Christ!

DAY 202

FEBRUARY 18

Answered Prayer

St. Mark 11:24 (KJV)

> *Therefore I say unto you, What things soever ye desire, when ye pray, believe that ye receive them, and ye shall have them.*

Do you remember that God places desires in your heart? Yes, He does. To see the manifestation of those desires you should (i) acknowledge the desires, (ii) pray that the desires be fulfilled and (iii) believe that you receive the desires. Each time you go to God in prayer about those desires believe that you have whatever they are. Do not be like some people and say something like, "If it is Your will". Use the formula as is in the Word of God and you will see wonders.

PRAYER: Lord, please help me not to doubt when I pray. Please help me to believe that I receive the things I ask You for in the name of Jesus. Amen

DAY 203

FEBRUARY 19

With My All

St Mark 12:30 (KJV)

And thou shalt love the Lord thy God with all thy heart, and with all thy soul, and with all thy mind, and with all thy strength: this is the first commandment.

It is love for God that will cause you to reverence Him with your whole being. Only His love that was pour into your heart can enable you to honour our sovereign Lord in this way. When we think of all the advantages that God has given us, it should be our strongest desire to please him. Let us therefore direct our whole being to giving Him reverence. Even as it seems daunting, all we have to do is ask Him to enable us. So we petition, "O God, grace to love You with all my heart, soul, mind and strength".

PRAYER: Lord, please teach me how to love You with my entire being.

FEBRUARY 20

Gratitude to God

Psalm 116:12-14 (KJV)

> *What shall I render unto the* Lord *for all his benefits toward me?*
>
> *I will take the cup of salvation, and call upon the name of the* Lord.
>
> *I will pay my vows unto the* Lord *now in the presence of all his people.*

How great must have been the trouble that God delivered the Psalmist from! Do you notice that he was not only grateful for the large blessings? He was grateful for all God's blessings, including the common, small ones. His heart appears to have been overwhelmed by God's kindness. Sometimes people fail to see God's kindness and instead ascribe their accomplishments to their own efforts. Never fall into that trap. The good things that God does for you are many. How will you ever repay Him for those good things? Can you even repay Him? Yes, it is possible to an extent. The best way, as David said, is to accept His gift of eternal life and pay all your vows (the things you promised Him you would do if ...)

DECLARATION: God has provided many things for me in abundance. I am grateful and to show my gratitude I accept His gift of salvation and pay my vows.

DAY 205

FEBRUARY 21

Show Favour

Psalm 112:5 (KJV)

> *A good man sheweth favour, and lendeth: he will guide his*
> *affairs with discretion.*

The teenage years are times when children become mean to others because they want to fit in a group or because they do not think the other person is pretty enough. Do not be part of that group. Make a decision to change, to become a good person by showing favour to others. As you grow older, I pray that God will make you able to lend and grace will make you willing to lend. May you meticulously manage your finances so that you will never find it necessary or desirable to borrow.

DECLARATION: In my interaction with my peers I will be generous and kind. I will lend to others. I will meticulously manage my finances.

FEBRUARY 22

Unfathomable Love

St. John 3:16 (KJV)

> *For God so loved the world, that he gave his only begotten*
> *Son, that whosoever believeth in him should not perish, but*
> *have everlasting life.*

God loves us. When Adam disobeyed God, sin entered the world. Satan thought that it would be the end of mankind however, God had a plan. Someone was willing to leave heaven, come to earth and die for Adam's fallen race. His name was Jesus. So, God sent Jesus to die on the cross, to buy us back from sin, so that we can have eternal life. How thoughtful and gracious God is!

PRAYER: Father, I thank You for the gift of eternal life through Jesus Christ.

FEBRUARY 23

Power to Become

St. John 1:12 (KJV)

> *But as many as received him, to them gave he power to become the sons of God, even to them that believe on his name*

The ability to gain the power to become God's child is available to everyone. This is so because there is an open invitation which is to 'as many as would receive Him'. Jesus is God's child. The day you asked Jesus to live in your heart He gave you the power to become God's child too. That means you have the authority to do the same things Jesus did. Will you begin to use that power?

CONFESSION: I received Jesus as Lord and Saviour of my life therefore I received the power to become God's child. I use that power for His glory.

DAY 208

FEBRUARY 24

Multiplication Through Thanksgiving

St. John 6:11 (KJV)

> *And Jesus took the loaves; and when he had given thanks, he distributed to the disciples, and the disciples to them that were set down; and likewise of the fishes as much as they would.*

Jesus prayed a prayer of thanksgiving before distributing food to His disciples who then distributed to the people. Five thousand men were fed with only two loaves and five fishes! Do you see any advantage of praying prayers of thanksgiving?

PRAYER: Lord, today I recognize the power of the prayer of thanksgiving. I will employ this prayer in my life. Thank You for this kind of prayer. In Jesus name, amen.

DAY 209

FEBRUARY 25

Bread of Life

St. John 6:46 (KJV)

I am that bread of life.

Bread is a staple. Staples are an important part of any meal; they provide energy. It is usually the largest portion of most meals. The Holy Spirit draws men to Jesus. It is our duty to hear the Holy Spirit and receive the grace that is being offered. Jesus Christ is the bead of life. John 6:46 is His testimony. He is the staple, the basic component, of life. He is the energy giver of your life. Spend time with Him so that you can have the energy to do all that is required of you.

DECLARATION: Jesus is the bread of my life.

FEBRUARY 26

Jesus' Tears

St. John 11:35 (KJV)

Jesus wept.

Jesus was overcome with sympathetic feelings when he was told of Lazarus' death. Those emotions resulted in him crying. Who are you sympathetic to? What moves you to tears? Sometimes we are overcome with grief and choke back tears but it is okay to cry. Tears help us see. They kill bacteria; remove toxins; build community and release feelings. Crying also lowers stress and elevate mood. As you go through life, always remember that there is no shame in crying as it is a very important part of our healing.

CHALLENGE: Make a list of the things you are passionate about, the ones that make you cry when you talk or think about them. For each item, state how you can correct it.

FEBRUARY 27

Mansions Await

St. John 14:2 (KJV)

In my Father's house are many mansions: if it were not so, I would have told you. I go to prepare a place for you.

There are many mansions in heaven. Jesus is in heaven where He is preparing a place for all who believe in Him. He promised to return for those who are in Him. We can hope in His promise. Even if others mock you for your faith, always remember that you have a glorious future in heaven.

CONFESSION: Jesus is gone to prepare a place for me.

FEBRUARY 28

Love God?

St. John 14:15 (KJV)

If ye love me, keep my commandments.

Do you love God? Have you been keeping His commandments? Here Jesus spoke to us in a very definitive and authoritative way. That is His will for those who love Him and His will is sufficient for those persons. When you keep Jesus' commandments you are proving that you love Him. Search the scriptures for His commandments. Highlight them and keep them.

CONFESSION: I love God therefore I keep His commandments. I love Jesus therefore I keep His commandments.

DAY 213

FEBRUARY 29

Spit and Clay

St. John 9:6-7 (KJV)

When he had thus spoken, he spat on the ground, and made clay of the spittle, and he anointed the eyes of the blind man with the clay,

And said unto him, Go, wash in the pool of Siloam, (which is by interpretation, Sent.) He went his way therefore, and washed, and came seeing.

This man had been born blind. He received his sight when he followed Jesus' instruction. You will agree that the remedy was rather strange. Who spits, makes a paste and uses the paste as a salve to heal blindness? While we do not know why Jesus used that concoction, He did and the blind man willingly allowed Him to administer it. Jesus is no longer on earth today but the Holy Spirit is. Divine healing is still available. The method that the Holy Spirit chooses to use may not be one that you are accustomed to or one that is recorded in medical texts. But, whatever method He chooses to use, trust Him to know of its potency. Whatever the Holy Spirit tells you to do, do it.

PRAYER: Father, please help me not to be skeptical of Your Word. Help me to do whatever the Holy Spirit tells me to do.

MARCH 1

Ultimate Obedience

Acts 5:29 (KJV)

> Then Peter and the other apostles answered and said, We ought to obey God rather than men.

The leaders of the city told the disciples to stop teaching in Jesus' name but they did not obey. They were placed on trial for their disobedience. When they were taken before the council (judges) to be judged, Peter explained that if they had to choose between the instruction of God and the order of men they would choose to obey God. God's laws are superior to those of men. All laws made by men should conform to the laws of God. Use the Bible as the reference to measure all laws.

PRAYER: Lord, please help me to always obey Your laws and not the ones men make that are in contravention of Your commandments.

MARCH 2

Obey the Instruction of the Holy Spirit

Acts 8:29 (KJV)

> *Then the Spirit said unto Philip, Go near, and join thyself to this chariot.*

The Holy Spirit speaks. Just as it is important to learn to hear the voice of God, it is also important to learn to hear the voice of the Holy Spirit. When you hear His voice be sure to obey His instructions. When Phillip obeyed the Holy Spirit one man was saved. Because of that one man the leader of a nation was saved. Do not be selective in your obedience to the Holy Spirit. You do not know what the ultimate consequence of your obedience will be. Likewise, you do not know what the ultimate consequence of disobedience to the Holy Spirit will be. Choose to obey.

CONFESSION: I listen to the voice of the Holy Spirit and obey Him.

DAY 216

MARCH 3

Power Through the Holy Ghost

Luke 24:49; Acts 2:2-4 (KJV)

> *And when the day of Pentecost was fully come, they were all with one accord in one place.*
>
> *And suddenly there came a sound from heaven as of a rushing mighty wind, and it filled all the house where they were sitting.*
>
> *And there appeared unto them cloven tongues like as of fire, and it sat upon each of them.*
>
> *And they were all filled with the Holy Ghost, and began to speak with other tongues, as the Spirit gave them utterance.*

God the Father. God the Son. God the Holy Spirit. God came to earth in the beginning. He made man and every day He visited him to talk. Man sinned and Jesus came. He dwelt among men until His death at Calvary. When He was resurrected from the dead, He went back to heaven. When Jesus left the earth the Holy Spirit came. He is the Spirit of truth, wisdom, understanding and revelation. He empowers Christians to do the work of God. The Holy Spirit lives in all who make Jesus their Savour. The Lord pours out the power of the Holy Spirit on those who desire it. He will do it just as He did on the day of Pentecost. Just ask Him.

PRAYER: O Lord, I pray for a fresh outpouring of the Holy Ghost upon my life. In Jesus name, amen.

DAY 217

MARCH 4

Prayer and Praise

Acts 16: 25-26 (KJV)

> *And at midnight Paul and Silas prayed, and sang praises unto God: and the prisoners heard them.*
>
> *And suddenly there was a great earthquake, so that the foundations of the prison were shaken: and immediately all the doors were opened, and every one's bands were loosed.*

Paul and Silas were beaten and imprisoned for preaching Jesus. While in prison they prayed and praised God and an angel opened the prison door. Years ago the church had midnight prayer meetings. Men, women and children would intercede at midnight. This was a regular feature of the Christian life. However, those prayer meetings are not so common today. Despite this, you can take your cares before the Lord at midnight. You can take hold of the horn of the altar as you petition God. It is very important that your prayers be accompanied by praise. You will be amazed at how it lifts your spirit and lifts you out dire situations.

CHALLENGE: Today pray and praise.

MARCH 5

Fight for Your Family

Genesis 14:14 (KJV)

> *And when Abram heard that his brother was taken captive,*
> *he armed his trained servants, born in his own house, three*
> *hundred and eighteen, and pursued them unto Dan.*

When kings waged war against Sodom and Gomorrah Lot, Abram's nephew, was taken captive. An escapee went and told Abram what happened to Lot. When Abram heard he went and fought against the people who had taken his nephew captive. It is important that you be willing to rescue your family from situations that will cause them to have an inferior quality of life. One way that you can do this is by fasting and praying for them. Another way is to plead the blood of Jesus over them. Whatever way is necessary, based on the situation, be willing to go in and fight for them.

DECLARATION: God is the author of salvation. I will fight in the spirit for any member of my family who has been taken captive by Satan.

MARCH 6

Cumulatively for My Good

Romans 8:28 (KJV)

> *And we know that all things work together for good to them that love God, to them who are the called according to his purpose.*

In 1997 I went to Church Teachers' College to do the Entrance Examination. There I met Shelly-Ann Shields and she quoted this scripture to me. Since then it has been an anchor scripture in my life. Think of all that has happened to you to date - the good and the bad. You can see how the good is working together for your good however, it is very difficult to see how the bad is going to work for your good. When you look back you will get a panoramic view of how both situations caused your growth, advancement and development. As a child of God you can be confident in the assurance that everything is working together for your good. The first part of this verse is often quoted by sinners and saints however; all things will only work for your good if you walk according to God's purpose.

PRAYER: Lord I thank You that all things in my life are working together for my good as I walk obediently in Your purpose.

MARCH 7

Christian Living

Romans 12:9 (KJV)

Let love be without dissimulation. Abhor that which is evil; cleave to that which is good.

The command to love is the overarching commandment. Here Christians are encouraged to love without deceit or pretense. We say that we love people but there is a lot of pretense and falsehood involved in out interactions with them. What if we were to love others as God loves us? What if we were to love as Jesus loves the Church? Indeed we would be loving without dishonesty. And, in doing so we would regard evil things with disgust. If you apply this command in your relationship with everyone you will see the positive difference.

PRAYER: Lord, please help me to love without deceit or pretense and to be repulsed by evil things, regarding them with disgust.

DAY 221

MARCH 8

Individual Accountability

Romans 14:11-12 (KJV)

> *For it is written, As I live, saith the Lord, every knee shall bow to me, and every tongue shall confess to God.*
>
> *So then every one of us shall give account of himself to God.*

Each person will be accountable to God. He is not going to ask your mother, father or best friend to give an explanation for your thoughts, words or deeds. You will have to give it for yourself. No doubt you have heard your parent say, 'Every tub must sit on its own bottom'. This means that you are responsible for your actions and must bear the consequences of those actions. So, live each day with this in mind.

DECLARATION: I am accountable for everything I do, I will do the work of God.

MARCH 9

A Living Sacrifice

Romans 12:1 (KJV)

> *I beseech you therefore, brethren, by the mercies of God, that ye present your bodies a living sacrifice, holy, acceptable unto God, which is your reasonable service.*

God no longer requires sacrifice of lambs or doves. Christians are required to place their lives on the altar as a sacrifice to demonstrate that all belong to God. Putting yourself on the altar means dedicating yourself to God. It also means being faithful in how you use your spiritual gifts. It is also to be humble and to live peaceable with all men. What are you consuming? How do you treat your "living sacrifice"? Are you filling it with God's word or negative music, ungodly literature and movies?

PRAYER: Lord help me to daily prepare and present myself to You as a living sacrifice, one that is worthy to remain in Your service through prayer and praise unto You. Help me to shun the things that will defile me "as a living sacrifice."

MARCH 10

Run!

Genesis 39:12 (KJV)

> *And she caught him by his garment, saying, Lie with me: and he left his garment in her hand, and fled, and got him out.*

The enemy will approach you with daily encouragement to defile yourself. He will try to do so when you are alone. He will tell you that if you indulge in sin no one else will know. But remember that if Joseph had had sexual relations with his boss' wife she would know and so would God. Joseph was trusted by his boss. You will be trusted by your parents and others. Do not succumb to any pressure, including that of your peers, to breach their trust. Remain faithful to God's instructions and stand boldly like Joseph and declare, "How can I do this great wickedness and sin against God?" God expects us to remain faithful unto Him.

DECLARATION: I will not engage in sexual immorality. I choose to run from sexual immorality.

MARCH 11

My Body: The Temple of the Holy Ghost

1 Corinthians 6:19-20 (KJV)

> *What? know ye not that your body is the temple of the Holy Ghost which is in you, which ye have of God, and ye are not your own?*
>
> *For ye are bought with a price: therefore glorify God in your body, and in your spirit, which are God's.*

Your body is a temple. The Holy Spirit lives in you – the temple. Incredible as it sounds, it is true - the Holy Spirit lives in you. You were bought back from sin with the blood of Jesus. This transaction means that you now belong to God. Because of this, whatever you do should bring glory to God. Since the Holy Spirit lives in you, you should make yourself a place that He will always want to be.

DECLARATION: My body is the temple of the Holy Ghost. I am not my own. I was bought with the blood of Jesus therefore I glorify God in my body. I will keep my body in a condition that is fit for a member of the Godhead to live.

MARCH 12

Overcoming Temptation

1 Corinthians 10:13 (KJV)

> *There hath no temptation taken you but such as is common to man: but God is faithful, who will not suffer you to be tempted above that ye are able; but will with the temptation also make a way to escape, that ye may be able to bear it.*

We are tempted each day. Every single day. Sometimes it seems that the temptation is irresistible but the scripture tells us that there is no exotic temptation. All of them are shared or experienced by other humans. Whatever temptations you are faced with know that God assessed them and determined that you are able to handle them. In His faithfulness God provided a way for you to escape the temptation long before you were confronted with it. When you are tempted, look for that escape. Do not yield. Be strong and say no, resist. God has an open door for you to escape through.

DECLARATION: I can overcome all temptation because God has assessed them and determined that I am capable of doing so.

DAY 226

MARCH 13

Growth

1 Corinthians 13:11 (KJV)

> *When I was a child, I spake as a child, I understood as a child, I thought as a child: but when I became a man, I put away childish things.*

You are expected to grow in your relationship with Christ. To grow in Jesus you should read the Bible, meditate (think deeply) on what it says, and fellowship with other Christians. You should also fast and pray. If you exercise these spiritual disciplines you will be sure to grow in God. As you grow you will being to see changes. One such change is that you stop doing some of the things you did when you just got saved. Enjoy the growth path.

DECLARATION: I grow in Jesus. As I mature in Him I stop doing childish things.

MARCH 14

Thank You

2 Corinthians 9:15 (KJV)

Thanks be unto God for his unspeakable gift.

God's gifts are numerous and diverse. When we stop to think of all that God has provided for us, saved us from and taken us through, we are continually astounded. When we think of the gift of salvation, afforded to us through the death of His son at Calvary, our hearts burn within us. Our heart swells with gratitude but we fail to find the words to express that gratitude. Yet, despite the limitations of language, we thank God for what we can and cannot articulate.

PRAYER: Lord, I thank You for the many different gifts that You gave me.

DAY 228

MARCH 15

Obey Your Parents

Ephesians 6:1 (KJV)

Children, obey your parents in the Lord: for this is right.

You are to obey your parents as long as their instruction is in keeping with God's Word. Sometimes you may not want to obey a parent because that parent is not in covenant with God however; the command is not conditional. It therefore means that you are to obey your parents even if they are unbelievers.

CHALLENGE: If you are not obedient, begin to obey your parents without questioning their authority for one week and journal your experience. At the end, assess the results and make a decision to continue being obedient. Pray to God to help you to keep this commandment.

DAY 229

MARCH 16

Honour Your Parents

Ephesians 6:2-3 (KJV)

> *Honour thy father and mother; which is the first commandment with promise;*
>
> *That it may be well with thee, and thou mayest live long on the earth.*

To honour your parents means that you are to love, respect, obey and reverence them. It also means that you are to respect and esteem them. They gave birth to you, fed you, provided shelter for you and love you in spite of your tantrums. God promises that if you honour your parents you will live long on the earth, you will not die pre-maturely. That's an awesome promise. Now, what will happen if you dishonor your parents?

DECLARATION: I choose to honour my parents.

MARCH 17

The Thinking Syllabus

Philippians 4:8 (KJV)

> *Finally, brethren, whatsoever things are true, whatsoever things are honest, whatsoever things are just, whatsoever things are pure, whatsoever things are lovely, whatsoever things are of good report; if there be any virtue, and if there be any praise, think on these things.*

Have you ever stopped to think about what you think about? Most of you have not. The truth is that your mind wanders without a moment's notice but you can train your mind, you can give it what to think about at various times. The Apostle Paul gave us the Thinking Syllabus in his letter to the Philippians. This syllabus outlines the things that you are to think about. Can you identify those things? When you do, begin to think about them. As you think about these thing you will develop a healthy mind and a positive attitude that will impact your whole life.

PRAYER: Lord, please help me to think on the things that Your Word instructs me to.

DAY 231

MARCH 18

It is Possible!

Philippians 4:13 (KJV)

I can do all things through Christ which strengtheneth me.

Paul experienced being in need and he experienced abundance. Having had both experiences he declared that he can do all thing through Christ who strengthens him. Whatever state we are in, God will strengthen us so that like Paul we can say, 'I am capable of doing everything because Jesus has strengthened me. There is nothing that I cannot do.'

DECLARATION: Declare Philippians 4:13 today and every day for the rest of your life.

DAY 232

MARCH 19

I Know Where It Will Come From

Philippians 4:19 (KJV)

> *But my God shall supply all your need according to his riches in glory by Christ Jesus.*

Adults sometimes spend a lot of time worrying. Worrying about finances, children and relationships. Do not get caught in that cycle. You get a jump start on life as you are learning this early. Paul was confident in God's ability to provide. God has not changed. By this assurance you do not have to worry about anything. God is your source. He will supply all your needs according to his riches in glory by Christ Jesus. When He does, use what He gives you wisely.

PRAYER: Lord I thank You for the assurance that You will meet my needs. I know that there is no limit to Your riches in glory, in Jesus name. Amen

DAY 233

MARCH 20

Grace-filled Speech

Colossians 4:6 (KJV)

> *Let your speech be always with grace, seasoned with salt, that*
> *ye may know how ye ought to answer every man.*

What are the things you say? Do they oppose sin? Is your speech courteous, respectful and gracious? If not, your speech is not being uttered with grace. It lacks charm, polish and refinement. Speech that is uttered with grace is polished. It is refined and charming. Such speech brings healing and joy to the hearers. Salt is an important seasoning that is added to food to enhance the flavours. When you speech is seasoned with this mineral that is essential for life, the lives of others will be tremendously blessed.

PRAYER: Pray for God to help you make your speech conform to this verse.

DAY 234

MARCH 21

An Attitude of Gratitude

1 Thessalonians 5:18 (KJV)

> *In every thing give thanks: for this is the will of God in Christ Jesus concerning you.*

Live your life with an attitude of gratitude. That is God's will for you. If you believe the Word of God and pray it, you will believe that every moment of your life is a piece of the tapestry that is being weaved in the fulfillment of His will. Despite how tattered any part of the tapestry may be at any one time, God requires that you give thanks. Be full of thanksgiving. And if you think that you do not have the capability to be thankful in the every situation, ask the Holy Ghost to assist you. He will enable you.

DECLARATION: In everything I give thanks to God. I will live my life with an attitude of gratitude.

MARCH 22

Tithe

Malachi 3:10-12 (KJV)

Bring ye all the tithes into the storehouse, that there may be meat in mine house, and prove me now herewith, saith the LORD of hosts, if I will not open you the windows of heaven, and pour you out a blessing, that there shall not be room enough to receive it.

A tithe is ten percent of a person's earnings. Tithing is the law that anchors prosperity. It guarantees your financial success. It is an investment in God. The Lord promises many blessings when you give a tithe. He will open heaven's windows and pour blessings on you. He will rebuke the things that eat away your resources. He will prosper you so much so that nations will see your prominence and call you blessed. I am sure that this is incentive for you to start giving your tithe now.

PRAYER: Father God, please give me grace to be an unceasing tither.

MARCH 23

Don't Want to Work?

2 Thessalonians 3:10 (KJV)

> *For even when we were with you, this we commanded you,*
> *that if any would not work, neither should he eat.*

During this season of life someone is responsible for your wellbeing. That person is ensuring that you get an education which will enable you to either start and manage your own business or become gainfully employed. By doing this they are laying a very important foundation. They are giving you the tools to become self-sufficient in adulthood. That is, they are empowering you with the skill-set to earn a living. One of the worst things is to see adults who refuse to work. Remember that the scripture says that if you become an adult and refuse to work you should starve. Promise yourself that you will be an industrious adult.

PRAYER: Lord, please help me to be a diligent worker, in Jesus name. Amen

MARCH 24

Pray

1 Timothy 2:1 (KJV)

> *I exhort therefore, that, first of all, supplications, prayers, intercessions, and giving of thanks, be made for all men;*
>
> *For kings, and for all that are in authority; that we may lead a quiet and peaceable life in all godliness and honesty.*
>
> *For this is good and acceptable in the sight of God our Saviour*

Can you pray? Please petition God for all men. Plead on their behalf. In verse two you are mandated to pray for kings (kings, queens, prime ministers and presidents) and all leaders. Stand before God and negotiate on their behalf. Let your voice be heard praying that they will accept the gift of salvation and that they will grow in the knowledge of Jesus. Ask God to give them wisdom. Pray and that they will lead selflessly. This will cause peace to be in your nation. You and your family will live without having to experience the terror of civil war.

CHALLENGE: Place the leaders of your nation persons on your prayer list. Pray for them constantly.

MARCH 25

Stir Up The Gift

2 Timothy 1: 6 (KJV)

> *Wherefore I put thee in remembrance that thou stir up the gift of God, which is in thee by the putting on of my hands.*

Timothy may have needed some encouragement about something for Paul to remind him of the gifts of God which were in him. Maybe he was doubtful of his ability to operate in those gifts. The gifts of God are things He freely gives to man. In Timothy's case, gifts were given to him when anointed men laid their hands upon him. God has given gifts to you. You have the spirit of boldness, power, love, and a sound mind: (See 2 Tim 1:6). The gifts of God are yours. Use them. Make them active and evident in your life.

PRAYER: Father, please help me to use the gift that You have given me to benefit others.

MARCH 26

Study!

2 Timothy 2:15 (KJV)

> *Study to shew thyself approved unto God, a workman that needeth not to be ashamed, rightly dividing the word of truth.*

Children of God are required to study to please God, not men. Most time if we please men we fail to please God. This is because men do not necessarily require the same things that God does. You are in school. School requires diligence, patience and application. At the end of your time in school will you be proud or ashamed of your accomplishments? If you want to be proud of your achievements you must spend time studying. Apply yourself to doing each task with excellence. Each completed task is a building block for success.

CHALLENGE: Decide to do the things that will make you proud when your time in school is over.

DAY 240

MARCH 27

2 Timothy 2:22 (KJV)

> *Flee also youthful lusts: but follow righteousness, faith, charity,*
> *peace, with them that call on the Lord out of a pure heart.*

During the teenage years, as hormonal changes occur, both males and females experience strong sexual desires (lust), for members of the opposite sex. The consequences of pursuing such desires are varied. The consequences are more than you can deal with at this stage of life. Paul admonishes Timothy to run away from this dangerous situation. That advice is as good today as it was then. Run away from youthful lust. The time will come when you will be able to explore those feelings. Do not believe your peers who tell you that you will die or that you are missing out. God will make the wait worth it.

DECLARATION: I will run away from youthful lust.

DAY 241

MARCH 28

Know Scriptures

2 Timothy 3:15 (KJV)

> *And that from a child thou hast known the holy scriptures, which are able to make thee wise unto salvation through faith which is in Christ Jesus.*

Do you know the scriptures? If not, today is a good day to start learning them. Aim to become conversant with the scriptures. They have the power to give you wisdom so that you will be saved from making mistakes, from suffering heartaches and living in lack. The Holy Spirit will reveal the meaning of those scriptures to you and as you apply them you will experience peace, increase and satisfaction.

PRAYER: Lord, I commit to remembering the scriptures. Please empower me to do so. I know that as I memorize scriptures they will make me 'wise unto salvation through faith which is in Christ Jesus', in Jesus name, amen.

MARCH 29

Purpose of the Scriptures

2 Timothy 3:16 (KJV)

> *All scripture is given by inspiration of God, and is profitable for doctrine, for reproof, for correction, for instruction in righteousness*

The Word of God has four purposes – a) it teaches (doctrine), b) it reprimands (reproof), c) it corrects errors or inaccuracies (correction) and d) it gives detailed information on how things are to be done (instruction). If you allow the Word of God to have full effect in your life you will never have any regret. The outworking of the four purposes will cause you to grow in grace, becoming more and more like Christ each day.

DECLARATION: The Word of God is for doctrine, reproof, correction and instruction. I will humble myself to learn the doctrine, to be corrected, reprimanded and instructed.

MARCH 30

Your Spiritual Heritage

2 Timothy 1:5 (KJV)

> *When I call to remembrance the unfeigned faith that is in thee, which dwelt first in thy grandmother Lois, and thy mother Eunice; and I am persuaded that in thee also*

Real faith was in Timothy. It had been passed down from generation to generation. It was part of his spiritual heritage. Do not forsake your spiritual heritage. If you do not have a spiritual heritage, create one by praying for your family and the unborn generation (the children you will have in the future). Be the change maker. Abraham had faith and followed God when no one else in his family did so. God promised Him many things including a generation that is as countless as the stars.

PRAYER: Heavenly Father, help me be a change maker, to believe You. Help me to have faith in You to carry me through school and be a success in my family. Help me to be determined to trust in You always and leave a successful spiritual heritage for my family, in Jesus name. Amen

DAY 244

MARCH 31

Can Others Tell of Your Love and Faith?

Philemon 1: 5 (KJV)

> *Hearing of thy love and faith, which thou hast toward the
> Lord Jesus, and toward all saints*

What kind of life can someone lead so that others speak of his faith in God
and love towards others? Such a person must have had firm faith in God.
He must have demonstrated the love of Christ to his Christian brothers.
Can those who know you speak well of your faith in God? Can they speak
well of and your love for Him and other Christians? This is a goal that all
Christians should aspire to.

PRAYER: Lord let me represent You where I am so those around will
know who You are and how faithful You are to me.

DAY 245

APRIL 1

Diligent Attention to the Word

Hebrews 2:1 (KJV)

Therefore we ought to give the more earnest heed to the things which we have heard, lest at any time we should let them slip.

God spoke to us by prophets and by Jesus, His Son. The things that they said are very important. Those things are written in the Bible. You should know what was said. Not only that but you should 'take earnest heed' – pay careful attention to, study and apply what was said. Do not allow anything that the Lord says to you to get lost, do not allow it to slip. Treasure God's Word and apply them for the advancement of His kingdom and your personal advancement.

CONFESSION: I give diligent attention to the Word of God.

DAY 246

APRIL 2

Be Careful of Unbelief

Hebrews 3:12 (KJV)

Take heed, brethren, lest there be in any of you an evil heart of unbelief, in departing from the living God.

Unbelief can prevent you from enjoying God's blessings. In school it may be suggested in some subjects, like Science, that you should not believe in God because there is no evidence of His existence. Take a look outside and critically analyze how everything that you are seeing came into being. What are you using to see? How did that come into being? Be assured of your faith in God. He is real. Do not depart from Him. To do so would be extremely dangerous.

PRAYER: Lord, please cleanse my heart from any trace of unbelief.

DAY 247

APRIL 3

Encourage Other Christians

Hebrews 3:13 (KJV)

> *But exhort one another daily, while it is called today; lest any of you be hardened through the deceitfulness of sin.*

Life can become overwhelming. Sometimes we wonder whether we are doing what God wants and whether it will be worth it in the end. People gets discouraged and it is in those times that reckless decisions are made. We can help each other by encouraging one another. Commit to encouraging one Christian every day. This will help then to remain committed to Christ. It will also help you to build your faith. Start by encouraging one person today.

CHALLENGE: Encourage one Christian each day and journal your experience.

DAY 248

APRIL 4

Our High Priest

Hebrews 4:14 (KJV)

> *Seeing then that we have a great high priest, that is passed into the heavens, Jesus the Son of God, let us hold fast our profession.*

Jesus is our high priest. He is now in heaven sitting at God's right hand. He promised that He will return one day but nobody knows when. Therefore, cling to your declaration of faith in Him. Do not allow your faith to wane. Let Him return and find you full of faith.

PRAYER: Lord, please help me to continue in faith so that when Jesus returns I will go to heaven with Him, in Jesus name. Amen

APRIL 5

Jesus Experienced it Too

Hebrews 4:15 (KJV)

> *For we have not an high priest which cannot be touched with the feeling of our infirmities; but was in all points tempted like as we are, yet without sin.*

Jesus was tempted in all the ways that you and I are tempted and will ever be tempted, yet He did not yield to the temptation. Since Jesus did not sin when He was tempted you have the capacity to resist temptation. When you are tempted you can pray to God in Jesus' name and ask for help to resist. God also offers advice on how to overcome temptation. You should submit to Him and resist the devil.

DECLARATION: Jesus was tempted in the same way that I am tempted and will ever be tempted. He did not yield to the temptation. Because Jesus did not sin I can overcome the temptations.

APRIL 6

God Does Not Forget

Hebrews 6:10 (KJV)

> *For God is not unrighteous to forget your work and labour of love, which ye have shewed toward his name, in that ye have ministered to the saints, and do minister.*

God will not forget your work. He will not forget what you do in His name. He will not forget what you do for other Christians. Are you doing anything for God? Will God have anything to remember? Work for God. You have to make sure that He will have something to reward you for. God is not unrighteous. He will not forget the work that you do in advancing the Kingdom. He will not forget the work that you do to assist the poor and infirmed. He will not forget the work that you do among the orphans and widows. He will not forget the work that you do in evangelizing. He is not unrighteous. He will not forget. He will reward you.

CHALLENGE: Make a list of the things you can do for other Christians. Begin to do them.

DAY 251

APRIL 7

Nothing Greater

Hebrews 6:13 (KJV)

For when God made promise to Abraham, because he could swear by no greater, he sware by himself

God promised Abraham that He would bless him and multiply his offsprings as the stars of heaven and the sand of the seashore. He also promised that Abraham's offsprings would be a blessing to every country on earth. God is sovereign. He is the only God. Because He is the only God, when He made the promise to Abraham there was no one greater for Him to appeal to so He swore by Himself. He pledged His power to fulfill the promise. What an amazing God!

PRAYER: Lord, thank You for Your promises. I am an heir to the promise You made to Abraham. I thank You that You swore by Yourself to fulfill that promise. I know that according to Your Words my offsprings will be a blessing to all nations.

APRIL 8

Endure to Receive

Hebrews 6:15 (KJV)

> *And so, after he had patiently endured, he obtained the promise.*

Sometimes you want God to fulfill His promise now, instantly. We want to dictate how He should work and the pace at which He should do it. However, we have to exercise patience. There is time between the making of the promise and its fulfilment. That time is for you to patiently endure so that when you receive the promise you will be equipped to handle it. God does things in perfect timing so His timing is never off, no matter how it may seem to you.

PRAYER: Heavenly Father help me to patiently wait for Your promises to be fulfilled in my life.

DAY 253

APRIL 9

Do Not Throw Away Your Confidence

Hebrews 10:35 (KJV)

> *Cast not away therefore your confidence, which hath great recompence of reward.*

Do not throw away or neglect your confidence in God. When you start anything knowing that God is faithful to His promise you are more likely to successfully complete it. During the hard periods you can hold on to the knowledge that what God said is your reality. If you forget that, you are likely to become discouraged and may even abort the venture. Hang on to your confidence in God. You will be richly compensated for that confidence.

DECLARATION: I will be blessed because I have confidence in God.

APRIL 10

Fully Persuaded

Hebrews 11:1 (KJV)

> *Now faith is the substance of things hoped for, the evidence of things not seen.*

Present faith is being firmly persuaded that God will perform the things He promised us in Jesus Christ, the things we hope for. It is evidenced by the things we have not yet seen but which will soon materialize. What are you hoping for? Is it something God said you can have? Is it something God said you can become? Whatever it is, are you fully convinced that God will give it to you? If you are not, begin to work on full persuasion. Build up your faith. Remind yourself of who God is and confess it.

DECLARATION: I am fully persuaded that God will perform the things He promised.

APRIL 11

Faith is Necessary to Please God

Hebrews 11:6 (KJV)

> *But without faith it is impossible to please him: for he that cometh to God must believe that he is, and that he is a rewarder of them that diligently seek him.*

When you pray you must be fully persuaded that God will do what He has promised. If you are not fully convinced it will be displeasing to God. Faith, full belief that God will do what He has promised, is an important ingredient to having your prayer answered. Another factor that is necessary for having your prayer answered is believing that God exists. If you are wavering on any of these two things, work on getting yourself firm.

PRAYER: Father, help me never to doubt Your existence. Please help me to have faith in You. Jesus please pray for me as you prayed for Peter in St. Luke 22:31.

APRIL 12

Cheerleaders

Hebrews 12:1 (KJV)

Wherefore seeing we also are compassed about with so great a cloud of witnesses, let us lay aside every weight, and the sin which doth so easily beset us, and let us run with patience the race that is set before us,

Patience and endurance are important in running the race of life in Christ. This race is not a sprint, it is more like a marathon. Many are cheering you on. Reject and resist sin as it will only condemn you, making it hard to endure the race. Sin is heavy. It weighs you down. It prevents you from putting your best foot forward. In the race of life, keep your eyes focused on Jesus. Do not get distracted by studies. Remember that His race required His blood; ours does not therefore, it is a much easier race. Run the Christian race with patience. You are guaranteed, by the blood of Jesus, to win. Those who are in heaven are cheering you on.

CONFESSION: I set aside the weights of life and run the race that is before me.

DAY 257

APRIL 13

Developing Patience

James 1:3 (KJV)

Knowing this, that the trying of your faith worketh patience.

Have you ever heard an adult say, "Don't try my faith"? Usually that statement is made in a threatening, no-nonsense manner. However, the testing of one's faith is not a bad thing. We all have stories of times when we were impatient and the embarrassment that it caused us. We can all work on our patience. When faith is tested patience is developed. Patience is a virtue that is necessary for a successful life. Whether you will be a servant or a CEO, patience is a necessary virtue.

PRAYER: Lord, thank you helping me to develop my patience.

DAY 258

APRIL 14

Ask for Wisdom

James 1:5 (KJV)

> *If any of you lack wisdom, let him ask of God, that giveth to all men liberally, and upbraideth not; and it shall be given him.*

Wisdom is a quality that every human being should desire. It is being wise and exhibiting good judgment. All adults can, if they are honest, recount things to you that they wish they had not done. They will tell you that if they exercised sensible or wise thinking they would never have done it. God gave Isaiah wisdom so much so that he spoke as a leaned person. It is said that God gave Him the tongue of the learned (See Isaiah 50:4). Examine yourself. Do you see where there is need for God's wisdom? Ask God to give it to you. Ask out of a pure heart. Do not make the request because you want to use the gift of wisdom in a conceited way. If you ask Him out of a pure heart, God will give it to you in large amounts. He will not express disapproval of your request. God will always give wisdom to those who ask Him out of a pure heart.

PRAYER: Lord, please give me wisdom.

DAY 259

APRIL 15

Help Thou My Unbelief

James 1:6 (KJV)

> *But let him ask in faith, nothing wavering. For he that wavereth is like a wave of the sea driven with the wind and tossed.*

The key to answered prayers is faith. Without faith you will not please God. In fact, the Bible says that it is impossible to please Him without faith! So, to have your prayers answered, you must pray in faith. If you are prone to doubting that your prayers will be answered, so ask God to help you to develop faith. Remember the father whose son was possessed? When he went to Jesus to ask that his son be healed Jesus told him that all things were possible if he could believe. The father responded saying that he believed but in the same breath asked Jesus to help his unbelief. (See St. Mark 9:20-24). If you need to, ask God to remove unbelief from you completely.

DECLARATION: I pray in faith, believing. I do not doubt.

APRIL 16

Enduring Temptation

James 1:12 (KJV)

> *Blessed is the man that endureth temptation: for when he is tried, he shall receive the crown of life, which the Lord hath promised to them that love him.*

Humanity has been afflicted by temptation since the day of Jesus. When we became Christians we were not insulated from temptation so we still get the urge to engage in things. The Christians' temptation is to do evil. Satan has not relented in his pursuit of your soul. Temptation can be intense and for extended periods. In such seasons of life, you will have to endure it graciously. In enduring, resist the devil: (See James 4:7-10). It is important that you have a good attitude as you endure temptation. A good attitude will help you to successfully endure. Remember that Job refused to curse God: (See Job 2:9). If you successfully resist it you will receive the promised crown from God.

DECLARATION: I successfully endure temptation.

APRIL 17

God Does Not Tempt

James 1:13 (KJV)

> *Let no man say when he is tempted, I am tempted of God: for God cannot be tempted with evil, neither tempteth he any man*

God would never draw you away from righteousness therefore God would never tempt you. In fact, God does not tempt anyone. He allows temptation, to an extent, but He does not tempt. Why does He allow temptation? Because temptation is a necessary character builder. It strengthens us for the great service that He has for us to do.

PRAYER: Lord, help me to see the character building opportunities in every temptation.

APRIL 18

Good Gifts

James 1:17 (KJV)

> *Every good gift and every perfect gift is from above, and cometh down from the Father of lights, with whom is no variableness, neither shadow of turning.*

God, the Father of lights, is the source of all good gifts. Unlike the sun which rises and sets and does not shine on all parts of the earth at the same time, God is always the same. Despite the seasons or the time of the year, He does not change. He is the same as He was before the earth was created, before time began. He will be the same at the end of time. God gave good gifts to man. God is still giving good gifts to man. Can you identify any good gifts in your life? Take time to thank Him for them.

PRAYER: Lord, today I thank you for _____. I know that You are the giver of every good and every perfect gift. Father, I thank You for the gift of consistency. Thank You for not changing. By not changing You allow me to have surety and confidence in You. Blessed be Your holy name, amen.

APRIL 19

Do the Word

James 1:22 (KJV)

But be ye doers of the word, and not hearers only, deceiving your own selves.

Many people hear the Word but fail to apply the principles and carry out the instructions. They fail to be doers of the Word. To be a doer of the Word you must: a) apply the principles which the Bible contains, b) follow the instructions and c) humble yourself to be instructed, corrected and reprimanded by the Word. The command to be a doer of the Word is a test of your obedience. When you do the Word you are saying by obedience, 'I trust You Lord'.

PRAYER: Lord, please help me to do the Word after I hear or read it, in Jesus' name. Amen

DAY 264

APRIL 20

Equal Treatment

James 2:1 (AMP)

> *My brethren, pay no servile regard to people [show no prejudice, no partiality]. Do not [attempt to] hold and practice the faith of our Lord Jesus Christ [the Lord] of glory [together with snobbery]!*

Do not prefer one person above another simply because he or she is rich or is able to create opportunities for you. Likewise, do not despite a person simply because he or she is poor. If you do, it is a sin. Civil respect must be given to each individual. In fact, standing in life should not determine how we treat a fellow believer, or anyone for that matter. Remember that the royal law is that we love our neighbor as we love ourselves.

PRAYER: Lord, help me to treat everyone as Your child.

APRIL 21

The Tongue

James 3:8 (AMP)

> *But the human tongue can be tamed by no man. It is a restless (undisciplined, irreconcilable) evil, full of deadly poison.*

The tongue brings blessings. It brings joy. However, the tongue is also the bringer of curses and death. It brings hurt and ruin. Think about the things you say when you get angry. Think about the things that are said about others while you were in cliques at school and at church. You do not have the ability to control your tongue by yourself. Only through salvation can you attempt to do so. As you control what is in your heart you will begin to control your tongue because the tongue says what is in the heart. As a child of God seek His grace and assistance to tame your tongue.

PRAYER: Ask God to help you to control your tongue.

APRIL 22

Overcoming Temptation

James 4:7 (KJV)

> *Submit yourselves therefore to God. Resist the devil, and he will flee from you.*

To overcome the temptations of Satan you must do two things:

i)   Submit to God – that is, yield to His authority; and
ii) Resist Satan – that is, withstand or counter his actions.

If you do none of the above things, Satan will use you as a beating stick; he will have his way with you. If you do one without the other you will not defeat him. To succeed you must do both – submit to God and resist the devil.

DECLARATION: I submit to God. I resist the devil. Therefore the devil flees from me.

APRIL 23

Do Good

James 4:17 (KJV)

> *Therefore to him that knoweth to do good, and doeth it not,*
> *to him it is sin.*

If you know to do good you have the obligation to do it. If you know to do good and fail to do it, it is a sin. Can you promote a good cause such as collecting food for needy families? Can you help to send the gospel to other places? Can you organize your youth group to do housework for a sick person? Can you organize a class visit to an orphanage or a children's home? Can you arrange a group of young people to read for the elderly at a golden age home?

CHALLENGE: Make a list of the good things you can do and do them one by one. Keep adding to the list as your ability increases.

DAY 268

APRIL 24

Be Prepared to Give a Reason

1 Peter 3:15 (KJV)

But sanctify the Lord God in your hearts: As you think about and be ready always to give an answer to every man that asketh you a reason of the hope that is in you with meekness and fear

Think of God in holiness, in awe. You will talk about Him in the same way that you think about Him. Those who hear you speak - classmates, teachers, acquaintances and others - will demand a reason or an explanation for your hope in Him. Do you know why you hope in God? If not, find out through reading the Bible and having a discussion with your parents, Sunday/Sabbath School teacher or your pastor. This will prepare you to provide an answer to those who enquire about your hope in God. Never be unprepared to speak of why you hope in God.

PRAYER: Lord, please help me to always able to explain the hope I have in You.

DAY 269

APRIL 25

1 Peter 5:6 (KJV)

> *Humble yourselves therefore under the mighty hand of God,*
> *that he may exalt you in due time*

Humility is abhorred in our society. It is scorned. Those who are humble are usually seen as weak because people often equate humility with weakness. However, it takes a strong and self-aware person to be humble. Show a low estimation of your importance under God's hand. When you do this He will raise you to a higher position in time to come. He gives grace to those who are humble.

DECLARATION: I humble myself to God's authority. I humble myself under God's authority.

DAY 270

APRIL 26

Increase of Grace and Peace

2 Peter 1:2 (KJV)

> *Grace and peace be multiplied unto you through the knowledge of God, and of Jesus our Lord*

Peter's greeting in this epistle reminds us that through our knowledge of Jesus grace and peace can be increased in our lives. The divine power of Jesus has given us all that relates to our existence and devotion to God. When Jesus called us, He made promises which we are the beneficiaries of. Some of His promises have conditions attached, others do not. Because of sin and our several human weaknesses, we need grace to see the fulfilment of some of His promises in our lives. By the divine power of Christ and a knowledge of Him we are able partake of His divine nature and His promises.

DECLARATION: Jesus has given me all things that relates to my existence and devotion to God through knowledge of Him. Through that knowledge I have been given exceeding great and precious promises through which I partake of His nature.

DAY 271

APRIL 27

2 Peter 1:5-7 (KJV)

> *And beside this, giving all diligence, add to your faith virtue; and to virtue knowledge;*
>
> *And to knowledge temperance; and to temperance patience; and to patience godliness;*
>
> *And to godliness brotherly kindness; and to brotherly kindness charity.*

The Christian life requires watchfulness. It requires careful and persistent work. To achieve the Christian character a person must carefully and persistently work the ways and means of being in constant communion with God. Faith, virtue, knowledge, temperance, patience and godliness are closely related graces that flourish together. The development of each of these graces in your life will help to keep you grounded in Jesus. They will also help you with your interpersonal skills.

CHALLENGE: Can you identify the nine virtues in the verses?

DAY 272

APRIL 28

2 Peter 3:9 (KJV)

> *The Lord is not slack concerning his promise, as some men count slackness; but is longsuffering to us-ward, not willing that any should perish, but that all should come to repentance.*

God fulfills His promises at an appointed time. He shows patience to us as His desire is that all men will enjoy eternal life. Sometimes the fulfilment of His promises seem long delayed. It is almost as if they will fail. I am sure that you have hear someone say that, 'I have been hearing that Jesus will return since I have been born and He has not yet done so.' Despite the seeming delay time is being given to all men to partake of salvation. It is a demonstration of His desire that all men be saved. Do you have a family member, friend or classmate who has not accepted Christ as Saviour? Evangelism is an area in which God welcomes our help. Share the gospel today and help God to see the fulfilment of His desire.

CHALLENGE: Share the gospel with an unsaved relative, friend and classmate today.

APRIL 29

Be Careful of Backsliding

2 Peter 3:17 (KJV)

> *Ye therefore, beloved, seeing ye know these things before, beware lest ye also, being led away with the error of the wicked, fall from your own steadfastness.*

It is possible for you, a Christian, to be led into error and fall from the unwavering, faithful and loyal way you followed Christ. This knowledge should make you more diligent in you pursuit of God. To prevent this from happening you grow in the grace of Jesus Christ: pray, practice biblical principles, follow biblical instructions, have daily devotions, attend Family Bible Hour, have Personal Word Time and fellowship with other believers at church. Be open and honest in your prayer because God knows all things.

PRAYER: Lord, please preserve me. Please do not let me be led away with the error of the wicked and thereby fall from my dedicated and resolute walk with You.

APRIL 30

Confess Your Sins

1 John 1:8 (KJV)

If we say that we have no sin, we deceive ourselves, and the truth is not in us.

The book of 1 John was written to Christians. We are reminded that we all sin from time to time and in fact, John reminds us that if we say that we have no sin we are involved in self-deceit. He goes further to say that if we make such a denial we are devoid of truth. We all sinned. We all sin. Jesus said He came to call sinners to repentance. Therefore if you say that you have no sin you are a liar and you make Jesus to be a liar. If we confess our sins, Jesus, who is faithful and just will forgive us all of them. He will also cleanse us from all things that are wicked, sinful and without virtue. Jesus came to call sinners to repentance. He made provision for our forgiveness so make use it.

CHALLENGE: Confess your sins to God.

MAY 1

Love for World vs. Love for God (I)

1 John 2:1-2 (AMP)

> *My little children, I write you these things so that you may not violate God's law and sin. But if anyone should sin, we have an Advocate (One Who will intercede for us) with the Father—[it is] Jesus Christ [the all] righteous [upright, just, Who conforms to the Father's will in every purpose, thought, and action].*
>
> *And He [that same Jesus Himself] is the propitiation (the atoning sacrifice) for our sins, and not for ours alone but also for [the sins of] the whole world.*

In the event that you commit a sin, Jesus has made provision for your forgiveness. When He died on Calvary His death was payment for all your sins – present and future. If you sin, confess it to Him. Like in a criminal case before the court, there are two advocates – one prosecuting and one defending. Satan is prosecuting. He is outlining everything that you did wrong. He is establishing the case to make sure that you are convicted. Jesus is the defence lawyer. He is the person who will put the case before God on your behalf, He is your advocate.

PRAYER: Jesus, thank you for being my Advocate.

DAY 276

MAY 2

Love for World vs. Love for God (II)

1 John 2:15 (AMP)

> *Do not love or cherish the world or the things that are in the world. If anyone loves the world, love for the Father is not in him.*

The things of this world have people of all ages loving them. Because people love the things of the world they also grow to love the world. Remember that you cannot love God and the world at the same time. You have to choose who to love, God or the world. Again, it is your choice. The Lord told the children of Israel that He had set life and death before them. Then He instructed them to choose life. They were to make that choice so that they and their children would live: (See Deuteronomy 30:19). Choose life; choose to love God and not the world.

DECLARATION: Lord I choose You, I choose life. I choose to love You Lord.

MAY 3

Mindboggling Love

1 John 3:1a (KJV)

> *Behold, what manner of love the Father hath bestowed upon*
> *us, that we should be called the sons of God:*

God's love for us is mindboggling. It is dumbfounding. Amazing love. Compassionate love. Condescending love. Exalting love. Patient love. Indescribable love. Immense love. Immeasurable love. What love! Imagine that we – fallen humanity – are acknowledged and treated by God as His children. By this acknowledgment we are His heirs and joint-heirs with his only begotten Son, Jesus Christ. A person receives all of this by simply turning to God in repentance and faith and living for Him in obedience.

PRAYER: Lord, thank You for Your love.

MAY 4

His Temple

1 Corinthians 3:16-17 (KJV)

> *Know ye not that ye are the temple of God, and that the Spirit of God dwelleth in you?*
>
> *If any man defile the temple of God, him shall God destroy; for the temple of God is holy, which temple ye are.*

Temples were holy places. They were usually splendid. In ancient times the cost of constructing one was very high and it usually took many years to complete. When we look at ancient temples today we are instantly in awe of the detailed architecture. Paul draws on this architectural reference to grand edifices to remind us that the Holy Spirit resides in us. Our bodies are the temple of God. Our bodies are valuable. Our bodies are holy. As such, do not use your body for anything that would displease God or that would make the Holy Spirit uncomfortable.

PRAYER: Lord, let me always be aware that the Holy Spirit lives in me. Let me act based on that awareness. In Jesus name, amen.

MAY 5

In His Image

Genesis 1:27 (KJV)

> *So God created man in his own image, in the image of God created he him; male and female created he them.*

You were created in the natural image of God. You were also created in His moral image. Sin defaced that image. However, when Jesus redeemed you by dying at Calvary you regained the ability to choose to conform to the will of God, to understand clearly, and to know wisdom. Your image was renewed! What will you choose to do with your new and unexplored abilities as a person who was created in God's image?

DECLARATION: I am restored to my original image because Jesus died for my sins on a cross at Calvary. I choose to use my redemption to honour God.

MAY 6

Rainbow Covenant

Genesis 9:13 (KJV)

I set My bow [rainbow] in the cloud, and it shall be a token or sign of a covenant or solemn pledge between Me and the earth.

After the flood destroyed the earth God made a covenant with Noah that He would never again use water to destroy the earth. The rainbow was the sign of that covenant. It is a beautiful emblem of mercy which sealed the covenant. Each time you see a rainbow it is a reminder of God's covenant. Rejoice and praise His name because He is faithful to His promises.

PRAYER: Lord, thank You for covenanting not to use water to destroy the earth again.

MAY 7

On His Terms

St. Matthew 4:19 (KJV)

> *And he saith unto them, Follow me, and I will make you fishers of men.*

Jesus came to save humans and to teach us how to be servants. His command to Simon Peter and Andrew was made without notice but they were prepared to obey it. When each disciple agreed to follow Jesus they did so on His terms, not on theirs. As a servant of Christ one of your primary duty will be soul-winning. Will you agree to follow Jesus on His terms? Will you agree to be a servant?

DECLARATION: I choose to follow Jesus on His terms. I agree to be a servant of Jesus.

DAY 282

MAY 8

Apparently Impossible

Genesis 17:16 (KJV)

> *And I will bless her, and give thee a son also of her: yea, I will bless her, and she shall be a mother of nations; kings of people shall be of her.*

Abraham, was ninety nine years old and Sarah, his wife, was eighty nine years old when God promised him that he and his equally old wife would have a son. By this time both of Abraham and Sarah were well past child-bearing years. The fulfilment of this promise seemed impossible however, God fulfilled His promise and Isaac was born to them. Isaac was born when Abraham was one hundred years old and Sarah was ninety. God's covenant blessings were reserved for Isaac and were later apportioned to him. No matter how long the delay in the fulfilment of God's promises, be assured that they will be fulfilled.

PRAYER: Lord, some things look impossible but I know that You can override impossibilities. You specialize in making what seems impossible possible. I surrender all the things in my life, especially those that seems impossible, to You.

MAY 9

He Knows Every Language

St. Matthew 6:7 (KJV)

> *But when ye pray, use not vain repetitions, as the heathen do: for they think that they shall be heard for their much speaking.*

Guess what?! You do not have to find fancy words to pray to God! In Jamaica the local dialect is Patois. As a child I spoke the dialect fluently and struggled with our official language. I use to think that I had to pray to God in English. However, I have since learnt that God understands every language and every dialect. When confronted by some situations I cry to Him in Patois and He answers. I even translate His Word into Patois and remind Him of it. He responds to my reminders. God understands and responds to His Word so pray them. In whatever language you pray, do not babble over your prayer. Do not use meaningless words. When you pray, always mean what you utter. Be careful that your prayers are not made so that you can be heard, seen and praised by men.

CHALLENGE: Do you have a local dialect? Pray to God in your local dialect. If not, remind God of His Word in your official language.

MAY 10

Prayer for Salvation

Genesis 18:20 (KJV)

> *And the LORD said, Because the cry of Sodom and Gomorrah is great, and because their sin is very grievous;*

Communities are in sin. Cities are in sin. Nations are in sin. Every Christian should be enthusiastic to see God's desire fulfilled. Therefore, we should all be praying for communities, cities and nations. We should be praying for Godly change to come to them and for the salvation of the inhabitants. We should always pray for missionaries and evangelists who share the good news of Jesus. And, we should pray that the people they speak to will accept the gift of salvation.

PRAYER: Lord, help me to always pray for the salvation of those who are living in sin. Help me to always pray for missionaries and evangelists.

MAY 11

The Bible, My Measuring Stick

St. Matthew 7:15 (KJV)

> *Beware of false prophets, which come to you in sheep's clothing,*
> *but inwardly they are ravening wolves.*

Not everyone or everything that calls on the name of Jesus is true. Listen keenly to every sermon and reference it against the Bible. Judge every religious book by the Bible's standard. Measure every statement against the Word. If they do not measure up you should reject them. There are people who have dedicated themselves to teaching a different gospel. Others have given themselves to tainting the things of God while others plant seeds of unbelief, designed to destabilize, through their statements. You have to be vigilant and watchful for these things. Remember that as children of God, we believe and are guided by what the Bible says about an issue. Anything outside of that is to be discarded.

PRAYER: Lord, help me to know your Word and Your voice so that I will not be led astray. Father, please help me to measure all that I read and hear by the Bible.

MAY 12

Jesus is in Tempestuous Situations

St. Matthew 8:23-24 (KJV)

> *And when he was entered into a ship, his disciples followed him.*
>
> *And, behold, there arose a great tempest in the sea, insomuch that the ship was covered with the waves: but he was asleep.*

Jesus was in the boat with His disciples while the storm raged. Even when things seem overwhelming Jesus is with you. He will deliver. The waves will not cause your boat to turn over. You will not drown. The great storms of life often end in clear skies. God is on your side. He will hear your cry and He will answer.

DECLARATION: Jesus is with me. My boat will not capsize. I will not be drowned by the storms of life.

MAY 13

Forever King

Psalm 10:16 (a) (KJV)

The LORD is King for ever and ever

God's kingship is forever. He reigns and will reign forever. There is not one person that will succeed Him – there is no heir to the throne of His Kingdom! There is no one that will overthrow Him. Satan tried it and he failed. When Satan tried, God did not even defend His kingship; angel Gabriel led the battle on God's behalf and Satan was defeated. No one can dethrone God. Jehovah's kingship is eternal.

DECLARATION: The Lord God is King forever and ever.

MAY 14

Acknowledge Jesus

St. Matthew 10:32 (KJV)

> *Whosoever therefore shall confess me before men, him will I confess also before my Father which is in heaven.*

Jesus is an advocate for all who confess Him before men, those who declare their faith in Him to others. In some cultures it is shameful for a person to admit that he knows Jesus. It is a disgrace for him to admit that he has relationship with Jesus. If he does great shame may come to him and his family. He may even be cast out of his community. Despite the shame, a believer in Christ should never deny Him. The consequence is too grave. If you admit to men that your faith is in Jesus, if you admit being in relationship with Him, He will admit knowing you – He will not deny you before God.

PRAYER: Lord, please help me never to be ashamed of Jesus. Help me to always acknowledge Him before men.

MAY 15

Lessons from Parables

St. Matthew 13:18 (KJV)

Hear ye therefore the parable of the sower.

Jesus taught many principles using parables. Parables are stories that are used to demonstrate a spiritual or moral principle. In order to understand the true meaning the reader has to look deeper than the literal meaning. In the parable of the sower Jesus tells of a sower who sowed seeds arbitrarily. Some seed fell at the side of the path with no soil, some fell on rocky ground with little soil, and some fell on soil which contained thorns. All of those seeds were either taken away or failed to produce a crop. However, the seeds that fell on good soil grew, yielding thirty, sixty, or a hundredfold: (See St. Matt.13:1-8). This parable demonstrates how industrious Satan is at snatching the Word from people's hearts and the responsibility that a person has to ensure that his heart is good soil. Would you like to go on a Parable Hunt?

CHALLENGE: Find all the parables of Jesus in St. Matthew, St. Mark, St. Luke and St. John. Find out the meaning of each. (You may invite your family to join you in this adventure.)

DAY 290

MAY 16

Offended By His Origin

St. Matthew 13:57 (KJV)

> *And they were offended in him. But Jesus said unto them, A prophet is not without honour, save in his own country, and in his own house.*

Many persons were offended by the humble birth of Jesus. They remembered that his father was a carpenter, a lowly profession. They did not want to learn from Him because they thought they were of equal or higher status. Today people reject God's chosen servants based on their career or lack thereof, the circumstances of their birth, or their social status. Remember that these are not bases for rejecting a man or woman who is walking according to God's will. It is a practice which you should consciously decide not to participate in. Despite their circumstances, receive those who have been anointed by God.

PRAYER: Lord even if my earthly family and community wrongly reject those You have called to lead, please help me to always honour them, in Jesus name. Amen

MAY 17

A Greater Purpose

Genesis 45:4-5 (KJV)

> *And Joseph said unto his brethren, Come near to me, I pray you. And they came near. And he said, I am Joseph your brother, whom ye sold into Egypt.*
>
> *Now therefore be not grieved, nor angry with yourselves, that ye sold me hither: for God did send me before you to preserve life.*

Whenever people do us wrong our first inclination is usually to call for revenge upon them. We seek justice on our own behalf. However, Joseph gave us a perfect example. His brothers sold him into slavery and as a slave he was lied on and thrown into prison but when he met them again he did not focus on their misdeeds. Instead he saw the greater purpose in what he had suffered. So, like Joseph, train yourself to see the greater purpose in every adversity. Be open to growing from each experience. Always look to see how God can be glorified through the situation presently or in the future.

PRAYER: Father, please help me to readily forgive and to see Your plan in every difficulty that I face. In Jesus name, amen.

MAY 18

The Reward

St. Matthew 19:27 (KJV)

> *And every one that hath forsaken houses, or brethren, or sisters, or father, or mother, or wife, or children, or lands, for my name's sake, shall receive an hundredfold, and shall inherit everlasting life*

I recently read a novel in which the grandfather provided for his grandson's university education because according to him, his son who became a pastor, 'chose the path of poverty'. Many people see following God's leading and doing His will as the path to poverty however, nothing could be further from the truth. There is abundance in grace. As God's children we enjoy the blessings of Abraham. In the blessing of Abraham is material wealth. In the covenant of God there is provision and eternal life. You will be rewarded for whatever work or sacrifice you do for Jesus. Keep being faithful to Him. He will provide all your daily needs and you will one day see the unimaginable beauty of heaven and enjoy eternal life.

PRAYER: Lord, I thank You for the promises of increase and everlasting life.

MAY 19

Jesus: The Passover Lamb

Exodus 12:21-22 (KJV)

> *Then Moses called for all the elders of Israel, and said unto them, Draw out and take you a lamb according to your families, and kill the passover.*
>
> *And ye shall take a bunch of hyssop, and dip it in the blood that is in the bason, and strike the lintel and the two side posts with the blood that is in the bason; and none of you shall go out at the door of his house until the morning.*

The children of Israel were required by God to do specific things in observing the first Feast of Passover. One of the things they had to do was kill a lamb and put the blood over the door post and the horizontal support at the top of the door. Today God no longer requires us to do this because Jesus became our Passover Lamb when he died on the cross at Calvary. But, we can apply the blood of Jesus. We can bring ourselves under the covering of the blood of Jesus and we can sprinkle the blood of Jesus on our doors. When we do, we will have the full benefits of His shed blood.

PRAYER: Jesus, thank You for becoming my Passover Lamb. Today I bring myself under the covering of the blood of Jesus. I apply the blood to every entranceway to my house. Lord, let the blood of Jesus speak on my behalf.

MAY 20

Heed Wisdom's Cry

Proverbs 8:1-2, 11 (KJV)

Doth not wisdom cry? and understanding put forth her voice?

She standeth in the top of high places, by the way in the places of the paths.

Receive my instruction, and not silver; and knowledge rather than choice gold.

For wisdom is better than rubies; and all the things that may be desired are not to be compared to it.

Wisdom is available to all. She is in a public and accessible place. She begs that her instructions be accepted. She is in the Bible, a path through which every Christian should journey daily, but not everyone acknowledges or accepts what is there. She continuously pleads that her instructions be accepted. Her instructions are better than silver, gold and rubies. Wisdom is better than all the things you could ever desire. Will you accept her?

CHALLENGE: Accept wisdom and understanding today.

PRAYER: Lord, today I hear wisdom crying and I invite her in. Come in wisdom. Dwell with me. I know that your instructions are better than gold, silver and rubies. Today I accept your instructions.

DAY 295

MAY 21

He was Humiliated for Me

St Matthew 27:30-31 (KJV)

And they spit upon him, and took the reed, and smote him on the head.

And after that they had mocked him, they took the robe off from him, and put his own raiment on him, and led him away to crucify him.

Imagine yourself being subject to public humiliation. Imagine people spitting in your face. Imagine them beating you in your head. Imagine your clothes being torn off. Imagine all of this happening in public. This is the indignity that Jesus suffered. Jesus suffered and endured this humiliation so that all humans can have eternal life by accepting the gift of salvation. Let us evangelize the world as it is God's desire that all men should be saved.

PRAYER: Lord, You gave Your only Son to be sacrificed at Calvary so that I can enjoy eternal life. I am grateful. Please help me to explain Jesus' sacrifice and its meaning to all who I come in contact with.

MAY 22

They Will Remember

Proverbs 10:7 (KJV)

> *The memory of the just is blessed: but the name of the wicked shall rot.*

The just man will die. The wicked man will die. 'What is the difference?' you ask. The difference is in how each is remembered. Even in death men will speak well of the just man. He will be remembered with joy. Honour and commendation will be attached to his name. However, the name of the wicked will be forgotten and if it is mention, it is spoken of with abhorrence. How will people remember you when you die? What will your eulogy say?

PRAYER: Lord, please help me to live a purpose accomplished life so that my impact on the earth will endure for many generations. I pray that even in death men will speak of me with honour and commendation. In Jesus name, amen.

MAY 23

Long Life

Proverbs 10:27 (AMP)

> *The [reverent] fear of the Lord [worshiping, obeying, serving,*
> *and trusting Him with awe-filled respect] prolongs one's life,*
> *But the years of the wicked will be shortened.*

In addition to honouring your parents, having reverence for God will prolong your life. The fear of the Lord will protect you from untimely death, whether by violence, disease or accident. The fear of the Lord is the highway to success. However, the life of those who do not fear God will be shortened. Today you have a choice to make – whether to fear God or not. Choose what is in your best interest. Choose to fear God.

PRAYER: Lord help me to reverence You because of who You are. Today I choose to fear You.

DAY 298

MAY 24

Signs to Jesus

Numbers 19:2-3 (KJV)

> *This is the ordinance of the law which the* LORD *hath commanded, saying, Speak unto the children of Israel, that they bring thee a red heifer without spot, wherein is no blemish, and upon which never came yoke:*
>
> *And ye shall give her unto Eleazar the priest, that he may bring her forth without the camp, and one shall slay her before his face*

Here the Lord required the children of Israel to offer a spotless heifer in atonement for their sins. The young female cow should not have been yoked. He should not have been subject to bondage. This spotless heifer represented the spotless Lamb of God – Jesus Christ – upon whom there was no bondage. The sacrifice pointed to Jesus' death at Calvary and His freedom in going to the cross. All through the Word the Lord points us to redemption through salvation. He gave us of His best. Let us do the same in return.

PRAYER: Lord I thank You for Jesus' sacrifice at Calvary. Thank You for helping me to see the Old Testament in light of the New Testament.

MAY 25

Promise Fulfilled

Luke 2: 36-38 (KJV)

> *And there was one Anna, a prophetess, the daughter of Phanuel, of the tribe of Aser: she was of a great age, and had lived with an husband seven years from her virginity;*

> *And she was a widow of about fourscore and four years, which departed not from the temple, but served God with fastings and prayers night and day.*

> *And she coming in that instant gave thanks likewise unto the Lord, and spake of him to all them that looked for redemption in Jerusalem.*

Prophetess Anna lived a life devoted to God. She was widowed seven years after her marriage and remained a widow for eighty four years. During that time she served God with prayer and fasting in the temple. She also encouraged the people as they anticipated the day Jerusalem would be redeemed. Prophetess Anna, who was of the tribe of Asher, Jacob's eighth son, had a promise from God. He promised her that she would see Jesus before she died. She had to wait approximately eighty four years between the promise and Jesus' birth but during that time she focused on her work for God and never gave up hope. After the apparent delay, God kept His word.

PRAYER: Father God, help me to hope in Your promises knowing that no matter what, no matter how long they take to be fulfilled, You will keep Your Word.

MAY 26

Not by Bread Alone

Luke 4:3-4 (KJV)

> *And the devil said unto him, If thou be the Son of God, command this stone that it be made bread.*
>
> *And Jesus answered him, saying, It is written, That man shall not live by bread alone, but by every word of God.*

Have you ever been tempted by sin to the point where it appears that you cannot think; the temptation has overtaken your mind? Imagine what Jesus must have felt when He was in the wilderness. He was ultra-hungry; He had not eaten in 40 days! At this vulnerable time in His life Satan tried to tempt Him with what He must have desire most – food. Despite being pulled towards something that appeared good and would have satisfied His flesh, He did not indulge. Satan will tempt you at your lowest moments. Be mindful of that fact and exercise the presence of mind and self-control that Jesus did. You have the mind of Christ.

CHALLENGE: Follow Jesus' example. Model Him.

DAY 301

MAY 27

All Night Prayer

St. Luke 6:12 (KJV)

> *And it came to pass in those days, that he went out into a mountain to pray, and continued all night in prayer to God.*

What a wonderful example! Prayer is our way of communicating with God. Still, it is a privilege that few of us take advantage of. Jesus is the Son of God yet He took time to pray. He did not pray for five minutes. He spent extended time with God. Here we see Him seeking God all night. He has a lifestyle of prayer. How often do you pray? Have you ever been to an all-night prayer meeting? How much time do you spend in prayer? Now is time to pray all night. Discuss it with your family. Talk to your youth leader about planning an all-night prayer session. Let it be a part of your life. Prayer is life changing. The destiny of humanity will be changed because you prayed. May you never be too busy or too tired to pray.

CHALLENGE: Plan an all-night prayer meeting with your family or with your youth leader. Be sure to attend the next all-night prayer meeting that will be held at your church. When you go, spend the entire time praying.

PRAYER: Lord, I thank You for the gift of prayer. I thank You for access to You. I will walk in the example of Jesus and the saints. I will come before You in prayer – I will be praying all night. Please strengthen me to pray all night. In Jesus' name, amen.

MAY 28

The Soil of My Heart

St. Luke 8:11-15 (KJV)

Now the parable is this: The seed is the word of God.

The Word of God is planted in the soil of your heart. In verses 12 to 15 we see the Word falling on different types of soil – different hearts. The ones by the wayside, where there is no deep fertile soil, where traffic is heavy the conditions are not favourable for growth and the devil snatched the seed of the Word before it even has time to impact its environment. While soils is made from broken down rocks, the Word which falls on rocks have no soil or shallow soil so it cannot take deep root. While the seeds of the Word may grow, they will not be sustained as the roots are not anchored. Other seed fall among thorns – the overgrowth which steals the sunlight and takes the nutrients, choking the seeds. These seeds cannot become trees and therefore will not bear fruit. However, there is good ground upon which the seed of the Word falls. When this happens it is nurtured with love and patience and after a time fruits will begin to appear. What kind of soil is your heart? What kind of soil is the Word being planted in?

PRAYER: Lord, I thank You that my heart is good soil. When I hear the Word I retain it and act upon it. The Word of God produces fruit in my life always. I thank You for this Lord. Blessed be Your holy name. Amen.

MAY 29

The Rod Corrects

Proverbs 13:24 (KJV)

He that spareth his rod hateth his son: but he that loveth him chasteneth him betimes.

God endorsed the spanking of children as a means correcting them. God's instruction is that the rod is to be applied to the child who is loved. However, today parents are told that they should not spank their children. The truth is that sometimes parents beat a child to the extent that it becomes abuse. This is not condoned. Boundaries are necessary for the development of character. Since no child is a saint, all will break the rules. So, when you break the rules you should expect to receive the agreed punishment. (In your spare time, research the outcome of children who are allowed to run wild without boundaries. Would you like to become as one of them?)

PRAYER: Lord I understand that as You discipline those who You love my parents discipline me because they love me. Please help all parents and guardians to understand the difference between discipline and abuse.

MAY 30

Forgive

St. Luke 17:3 (KJV)

> *Take heed to yourselves: If thy brother trespass against thee, rebuke him; and if he repent, forgive him.*

If another Christian does you wrong, you are to express your disapproval of his action. To do otherwise would be hypocritical. If when you have expressed disapproval he apologizes, you are to forgive him. An apology is the only price for forgiveness however, some people will not apologize. If someone who does you wrong refuses to apologize, you should forgive them nonetheless. Forgiveness is not for the offender, it is for you. It frees you. Remember that forgiveness breed bitterness. Bitterness will eat away at you.

DECLARATION: I unconditionally forgive those who have wronged me. I will forgive all who wrong me.

MAY 31

The Sun Stood Still, The Moon Stayed

Joshua 10:12-13 (KJV)

> *Then spake Joshua to the LORD in the day when the LORD delivered up the Amorites before the children of Israel, and he said in the sight of Israel, Sun, stand thou still upon Gibeon; and thou, Moon, in the valley of Ajalon.*
>
> *And the sun stood still, and the moon stayed, until the people had avenged themselves upon their enemies. Is not this written in the book of Jasher? So the sun stood still in the midst of heaven, and hasted not to go down about a whole day.*

God stopped the solar system so that the children of Israel could win a war! The sun stood still. This was the "impossible" but Joshua's prayer was an audacious one. He was running out of time. He needed extra daylight to win the battle. So, in view of those he led, he asked God for the seemingly impossible. What faith he must have possessed! The earth revolves around the sun giving us day and night so I think it is logical that the earth stopped rotating. Imagine that! This was not the only time that the working of the solar system was disrupted in answer to a prayer. Remember that God turned back time for king Hezekiah which meant that He had to reverse the rotational movement of the earth. Awesome God He is! Be encouraged - the crisis you face is not too hard for God to handle. He will make provision for your victory. Whenever you need to, ask Him to make the sun stand still on your behalf.

DECLARATION: I will trust in God who caused the earth to stop revolving around the sun. The sun stood still and the moon stayed. God will cause the sun to stand still on my behalf. He will make me victorious. Hallelujah!

DAY 306

JUNE 1

Parental Instruction

Proverbs 13:1 (KJV)

> *A wise son heareth his father's instruction: but a scorner heareth not rebuke.*

Sometime children 'zone out' their parents, especially when they are being corrected or reprimanded. However, as you see, it is foolish to do that. The wise child will listen to his parents' instructions and their expression of disapproval. He will also take steps to change the unbecoming behavior. In fact, when your parents' rebuke is received with a positive attitude you will consider it and change your behavior. This will result in you becoming a better person.

DECLARATION: I listen to and obey the instructions and correction of my parents.

DAY 307

JUNE 2

Controlled Speech

Psalm 141:3 (KJV)

> *Set a watch, O Lord, before my mouth; keep the door of my lips.*

Having difficulty with controlling the things that come out of your mouth? I use to be like that. In fact, during my teenage years I was very caustic and because of that I lost many friends. One day, while reading this verse I saw myself and asked the Lord to watch over my mouth. He did and things changed for me. If you are experiencing the same thing that I did you can ask God to assist you. When He is watching over your mouth and guarding your lips love will wrap all that comes from your mouth.

PRAYER: Lord, please help me with what I say by keeping watch over my mouth and guarding my lips.

JUNE 3

He's Incomparable

Psalm 86:8, 10 (KJV)

> *Among the gods there is none like unto thee, O Lord; neither are there any works like unto thy works.*
>
> *For thou art great, and doest wondrous things: thou art God alone.*

God is incomparable. He does wonderful things. Look at the beauty of creation. The baby blue sky with soft powdery wisps splashed across; the golden sunshine that bathes the earth in warmth. The azure sea contrasted against pearl white sand. The strength and mysteries of the oceans. Flowers of all shapes, colours and scents blanket the land. Mountains rise majestically. He heals. He restores. He rebuilds. He protects. He preserves. There is none like Him.

DECLARATION: There are no gods like You, O God. Your works are incomparable. You are great. You do astounding things. You are incomparable.

DAY 309

JUNE 4

Put the Word in Your Heart

Psalm 119:11 (KJV)

> *Thy word have I hid in mine heart, that I might not sin against thee.*

Hard times will come. Trying times are inevitable. Tempestuous times are seasonal. When these times come many people become faint. Many never prepared for them. One way to prepare is to meditate upon the Word of God. When we do this we commit the Word to memory. It becomes a part of us. When the Word of God is in our heart, when we have committed it to memory, the Holy Spirit will remind us of it when necessary. If we do not commit the Word to memory the Holy Spirit will not have anything to remind us of. Let us prepare for the days ahead.

PRAYER: O Lord God of heaven and earth, please give me a deep hunger for Your Word. Please help me to study and meditate on Your Word. Please help me to hide Your Word in my heart so that I can avoid sin.

DAY 310

JUNE 5

St. John 1: 41-42 (KJV)

> *He first findeth his own brother Simon, and saith unto him, We have found the Messias, which is, being interpreted, the Christ.*

> *And he brought him to Jesus. And when Jesus beheld him, he said, Thou art Simon the son of Jona: thou shalt be called Cephas, which is by interpretation, A stone.*

Andrew accepted Jesus' invitation to follow Him. The first thing that he did afterwards was to go in search of his brother, Simon. No doubt he wanted his brother to experience eternal life also. When he found Simon he introduced him to Jesus. Do you have family, friends and classmates who do not know Jesus? If yes, do like Andrew. Go and find them. Tell them about Jesus. Introduce them to Him. Help them to develop relationship with Him.

PRAYER: Lord, please help me love my family, friends and classmates enough to introduce them to You.

DAY 311

JUNE 6

Praise God

Psalm 150:6 (KJV)

> *Let every thing that hath breath praise the LORD. Praise ye the LORD.*

Oftentimes people do not praise. Their excuse is, "I can't sing". You do not have to be able to 'sing' to praise God. Psalm 100:1 says you are to make a **joyful noise** to God. Shout His praise! You can praise God on the instruments. You can praise Him in dance. Notice it did not say 'coordinated dance'. There is no excuse for failing to praise God. Praise brings God pleasure. It lifts your soul. Praise is also an effective weapon in warfare but we do not engage it.as we should. There is breath in your body. Open your mouth and begin to express your admiration of God. Praise Him.

CHALLENGE: Engage in a session of high praise today.

DAY 312

JUNE 7

Give God Your Best

St. John 12:3 (KJV)

> *Then took Mary a pound of ointment of spikenard, very costly, and anointed the feet of Jesus, and wiped his feet with her hair: and the house was filled with the odour of the ointment.*

Mary gave Jesus her best offering. It is said that the ointment cost a whole year's wages. Her act demonstrates selflessness in worship. It was a bold but humble giving. And, overwhelmed with gratitude and reverence, she wiped his feet with her hair. Such was her profound love for our Saviour. When her offering was given, it changed the entire atmosphere – the house was filled with its scent. What will you give to the Lord? What will your offering be? Will you give Jesus an offering out of gratitude and reverence for who He is?

DECLARATION: I will give my best offering to Jesus.

DAY 313

JUNE 8

Isaiah 7:14 (KJV)

> *Therefore the Lord himself shall give you a sign; Behold, a virgin shall conceive, and bear a son, and shall call his name Immanuel.*

Jesus was born about seven hundred years after Isaiah made this prophecy. Seven hundred years is a very long time. The persons to whom the prophecy was articulated would have died many generations before it was fulfilled. If Isaiah had not written down the prophecy its utterance would have been lost. In fact, many persons may have lost hope of seeing the Christ Child, the Saviour. The lesson from this is to write down every prophetic word that God gives you. If it is not fulfilled in your lifetime those who come after you will look for its fulfillment much like Daniel did: (See Daniel 9:2). God will fulfill every prophetic word.

CHALLENGE: Get a Prophesy Journal and record ever prophecy given to you. Record the date it is given and the date when each is fulfilled.

DAY 314

JUNE 9

Abiding in God

St. John 15:4-5 (KJV)

Abide in me, and I in you. As the branch cannot bear fruit of itself, except it abide in the vine; no more can ye, except ye abide in me.

I am the vine, ye are the branches: He that abideth in me, and I in him, the same bringeth forth much fruit: for without me ye can do nothing.

Jesus has offered those who accept salvation a safe place to live, in Him. He is the vine. If you, the branch, cut off yourself from Him you will not bear any fruit. However, if you accept the offer to abide in Him you are sure to bear fruit. God is the gardener and He cuts, trims and prunes to ensure that you will increase your yield - the amount of fruit produced. The key to fruitfulness is remaining in Jesus.

DECLARATION: I am the branch and I abide in Jesus, the vine. By abiding in Christ I am guaranteed to and do bear much fruit.

JUNE 10

Reverence His House

Habakkuk 2:20 (KJV)

> *But the LORD is in his holy temple: let all the earth keep silence before him.*

At least one day per week we gather in a building to worship God. That building is called the house of God because we gather there to worship Him. Despite the fact that it is the house of God, we sometimes forget how we should behave. When you enter God's house you should be reverent and prayerful. Turn your heart and mind towards Him. Remember that God said that He is wherever two or three persons are gathered in His name (See Matt. 18:20), so He is in the place where you gather to worship. As a mark of respect for Him: avoid incessant chatter; avoid cross talking and cross walking; avoid eating and sleeping. Be reverent.

DECLARATION: I will be reverent when I enter the house of God.

DAY 316

JUNE 11

Response To Your Enemies' Distress

2 Samuel 1:4; 12 (KJV)

> *And David said unto him, How went the matter? I pray thee, tell me. And he answered, That the people are fled from the battle, and many of the people also are fallen and dead; and Saul and Jonathan his son are dead also.*
>
> *And they mourned, and wept, and fasted until even, for Saul, and for Jonathan his son, and for the people of the* LORD, *and for the house of Israel; because they were fallen by the sword*

Saul, the king of Israel, searched for David to kill him but despite this David did not rejoice when he heard of his death; instead he mourned. How do you respond when bad things happen to people who are not fond of you? Might I encourage not to glory in their demise? In fact, Proverbs 24:17 tells us that if we rejoice at our enemies' demise the Lord will turn away His wrath from them.

PRAYER: Lord, please help me not to rejoice when bad things happen to people who are not fond of me. Let there be no gladness in my heart when they fall.

DAY 317

JUNE 12

Ezekiel 3:4 (KJV)

And he said unto me, Son of man, go, get thee unto the house of Israel, and speak with my words unto them.

Did you became a Christian because someone told you about the good news of Jesus? That's the way I got to know Him. A minister shared the gospel at a crusade at Mt. Hermon United Church in Lamb's River, Westmoreland. I was in 4th form (grade 10) at high school. Image if no one had shared that very important information with me. Image if no one had shared that very important information with you. Imagine what will happen to those who do not hear the gospel. Are you afraid of sharing the gospel? You do not have to be. When you share the gospel you are not responsible for the results, God is. You are only responsible for sharing.

CHALLENGE: Continue to share the gospel of Jesus Christ.

JUNE 13

Righteous Judgment

1 Kings 3:9 (KJV)

> *Give therefore thy servant an understanding heart to judge thy people that I may discern between good and bad: for who is able to judge this thy so great a people?*

As king, Solomon had to judge the people of Israel. This was a very important job. What he did could cause reconciliation or rift between litigants. His judgment could cause disquiet leading to civil unrest. King Solomon recognized the weight of this responsibility. He also recognized that he could not carry out this job in his own strength and based on his own intellect, so he prayed for God to give Him the capability to do judge justly. This was a humble position for King Solomon to take. God, seeing the sincerity of his heart, granted his request. One day you will be a judge. You may have to judge between your siblings, your peers or your children. Pray King Solomon's prayer in faith.

PRAYER: Pray that God will give the judiciary in your country an understanding heart to judge the people.

JUNE 14

I Am a Testimony of His Love

Daniel 6: 21-22 (KJV)

Then said Daniel unto the king, O king, live forever.

My God hath sent his angel, and hath shut the lions' mouths, that they have not hurt me: forasmuch as before him innocency was found in me; and also before thee, O king, have I done no hurt.

King Darius had commanded that Daniel be thrown into the lion's den. Lions are fierce creatures with a naturally voracious appetite. They devour their prey very rapidly. When in the wild, they usually hunt at night however; when confined, they eat the food given, including humans. It was logical that the lions would eat Daniel. King Darius was restless. He did not eat and he could not sleep that night. Early the next morning he went to the den to find out Daniel's fate. He hoped that God would rescue Daniel and indeed God had! Daniel was safe and sound. There will always be evidence of God's abiding love for His children who are faithful to Him. When God delivers you, be sure to give Him glory.

PRAYER: Lord, I know that because of Your love I will always be a testimony to others. Please help me to always be faithful to You, in Jesus name. Amen

DAY 320

JUNE 15

Acts 8:2-3 (KJV)

> *And devout men carried Stephen to his burial, and made great lamentation over him.*
>
> *As for Saul, he made havock of the church, entering into every house, and haling men and women committed them to prison.*

Saul was a learned man of the Jewish faith. He had been instructed by the best teachers and had become very zealous about upholding the law. In Acts 7:1-53 Stephen made an impassioned speech before the high priest and council members who, moments later, sanctioned his death. Saul approved Stephen's killing. In fact, the young men who stoned Stephen to death placed their coat at Saul's feet. Saul was so zealous that he led the persecution of the early church. However, God changed him (see Acts 9:1-19). This reminds us that no one is beyond the grace of God.

PRAYER: Lord I thank You for Your grace.

DAY 321

JUNE 16

In Their Footsteps

2 Chronicles 29:1-3 (KJV)

> *Hezekiah began to reign when he was five and twenty years old, and he reigned nine and twenty years in Jerusalem. And his mother's name was Abijah, the daughter of Zechariah.*
>
> *And he did that which was right in the sight of the LORD, according to all that David his father had done.*
>
> *He in the first year of his reign, in the first month, opened the doors of the house of the LORD, and repaired them.*

Hezekiah was only twenty-five years old when he became leader of Israel. That's a very young age to undertake that kind of responsibility but Hezekiah seemed to have been mature. He had a Godly mother and an ungodly father who worshipped idols and burnt his own sons as sacrifice to the idols. When he became the leader, Hezekiah had to choose which path he would take. He did not choose to ignore the example set by his mother and grandfather Zechariah, who no doubt taught his daughter the fear of the Lord. King Hezekiah led a great spiritual revival in his time, beginning with the opening of the doors of the temple. When placed in positions of leadership, will you follow the footsteps of your fathers in the faith?

PRAYER: Lord, please help me to do right in Your sight and to follow the example of my fathers in the faith. Show me the places in Your house that need repair and give me grace to do it, in Jesus name. Amen

JUNE 17

No Condemnation

Romans 8:1-2 (KJV)

> *There is therefore now no condemnation to them which are in Christ Jesus, who walk not after the flesh, but after the Spirit.*
>
> *For the law of the Spirit of life in Christ Jesus hath made me free from the law of sin and death.*

If you are in Christ and you walk after the Spirit you will not be condemned. What does it mean to be in Christ? It is to live, move and have our being in Him: (See Acts 17:28). So, the believer who is in Christ and allows the Holy Spirit to lead him cannot be condemned by the world. God may chastise, punish or reprimand him for any untoward act but the world cannot condemn him. In Jesus, by His grace, you are free from the law of sin and death. This is a liberating freedom constrained only by the Word of God!

CONFESSION: I am a child of God. I am in Christ. I walk after the leading and promptings of the Holy Spirit. I am an heir to the kingdom of God. Jesus redeemed me from condemnation and from death. I am not condemned! I am free from sin and death by the law of the Spirit of life in Jesus.

DAY 323

JUNE 18

Salvation of the Jews

Romans 10:1 (KJV)

> *Brethren, my heart's desire and prayer to God for Israel is, that they might be saved.*

God desires that all every human being be saved. In every nations there is at least one Christian. It is the duty of that person to use prayer to bring the will of God to pass. It is the duty of every Christian to pray for the salvation of his country. Have you been praying for your country? Paul greatly desired it. It was his deepest desire to see Israel saved. What is your deepest desire?

PRAYER: Pray for the salvation of your nation.

DAY 324

JUNE 19

Jesus the Leader

Colossians 1:18 (KJV)

> *And he is the head of the body, the church: who is the beginning, the firstborn from the dead; that in all things he might have the preeminence.*

Jesus is not the head of just one congregation or denomination. He is the head of all believers. He is the head of the Church. He is eternal. He is the first to be raised from the dead to immortality and because of this He is chief over all. Isn't it awesome to know that you are related to such a person? Indeed it is. He is your brother.

DECLARATION: Jesus is the head of the Church.

JUNE 20

Selflessness In The Days To Come

Esther 4:15-16 (KJV)

Then Esther bade them return Mordecai this answer,

Go, gather together all the Jews that are present in Shushan,
and fast ye for me, and neither eat nor drink three days, night
or day: I also and my maidens will fast likewise; and so will
I go in unto the king, which is not according to the law: and
if I perish, I perish.

The Jews were about to be killed. When her Uncle Mordecai sent a message to tell her of the looming disaster, Queen Esther had to make a decision between her life and the lives of her people. Should she go in to the king and risk death or should she remain quiet and hope that her life would be spared? She determined to do all in her power to assist her people. This meant risking her life. There will come a day in your life when you have to decide between yourself and the fate of others in the kingdom of God. How will you decide?

PRAYER: Lord, help me to be selfless in the work that I do for You.

DAY 326

JUNE 21

Rescued By a Fish

Jonah 1:3, 17 (KJV)

> *But Jonah rose up to flee unto Tarshish from the presence of the LORD, and went down to Joppa; and he found a ship going to Tarshish: so he paid the fare thereof, and went down into it, to go with them unto Tarshish from the presence of the LORD.*
>
> *Now the LORD had prepared a great fish to swallow up Jonah. And Jonah was in the belly of the fish three days and three nights.*

I love the story of Jonah. It always fascinates me that he tried to run away from the presence of God who is omnipresent. Even when we disobey Him God always has creative solutions to rescue us. O how He loves us.

PRAYER: Lord, thank You for your constant consideration and protection.

DAY 327

JUNE 22

Turn From Sin

Psalm 106:43 (KJV)

> *Many times did he deliver them; but they provoked him with their counsel, and were brought low for their iniquity.*

God delivered the children of Israel many times but they kept rebelling against Him. As a result they wasted away in their sin. The same thing happens when we rebel against God: we become fruitless. This is not a state for the child of God. If you ever find yourself here, you can get out by utilizing the provision of God – confess your sins and ask him to forgive you. Accept God's deliverance and repent, turn away from evil. If you do not turn away, you will waste away like the children of Israel did.

CHALLENGE: Accept God's provision of forgiveness. Say, 'Lord, I accept Your forgiveness'

DAY 328

JUNE 23

Turn From Evil

Micah 2:1 (KJV)

> *Woe to them that devise iniquity, and work evil upon their beds! when the morning is light, they practise it, because it is in the power of their hand.*

Today's society glamourize evil. It is customized and packaged for every age group. Interest groups try to create buy-in by making it part of the popular culture. However, a fascination with evil is not good. Constantly thinking about it is not good. Dabbling in evil is a rejection of God. There is a 'woe' to people who conceptualize and engage in wickedness. The warning is given because those who entertain the fascination with evil find themselves doing it, sometimes without even giving a conscious thought.

PRAYER: Lord, please help me not to think of evil things. I do not want to think about them because they will push me to do evil. Father please let Your Word cleanse my thoughts. Let Your Word neutralize and erase every evil thought from my mind.

DAY 329

JUNE 24

In the Face of Death

Daniel 6:10 (KJV)

> *Now when Daniel knew that the writing was signed, he went into his house; and his windows being open in his chamber toward Jerusalem, he kneeled upon his knees three times a day, and prayed, and gave thanks before his God, as he did aforetime.*

Daniel's counterparts were jealous of him. They devised a scheme to entrap him and it worked! They advised King Darius to sign a decree that anyone who prayed to any god within 30 days would be punished. It was widely known that Daniel prayed at his window towards Jerusalem three times daily. When the king's decree was issued Daniel did not change his prayer habits. Instead, he allowed his convictions to guide him and God honoured his commitment. What would you do if you are told to deny that Jesus is Lord or be killed?

PRAYER: Lord, I want to be so convinced of You that even when faced with death I will choose to die instead of denying or disobeying You.

JUNE 25

Love

1 Corinthians 13:1 (KJV)

> *Though I speak with the tongues of men and of angels, and have not charity, I am become as sounding brass, or a tinkling cymbal.*

Love is the base character trait of all Christians. The Holy Spirit has poured God's love into our hearts. This deposit of love enables us to love others. Here Paul reminds us that our speech should be wrapped in love. This is very important because no matter how eloquent your speech, if it is uttered without love, it will only aggravate the hearer. Many persons hear the truth but reject it because it was not stated in love. If you have all other Christian traits without love it will not be of any value to you or to others.

PRAYER: Lord, I thank You that the Holy Spirit poured out Your love into my heart. Please help me to do everything, even the most difficult things, in love. Please help me to love others as You love me, in Jesus name. Amen

DAY 331

JUNE 26

Pray for Your Accusers

Job 42:10 (KJV)

> *And the LORD turned the captivity of Job, when he prayed*
> *for his friends: also the LORD gave Job twice as much as he*
> *had before.*

Job suffered deep pain and affliction. Satan killed his children. Job lost his property. He suffered extreme physical pain due to sickness. During his suffering Job was visited by some friends. Their intention was to comfort him but they ended up questioning his integrity before God and accusing him of transgressions. However, Job maintained his innocence. Despite Job's denial of sin, God did not relieve him then. Job did not know the reason for his trials but he continued to trust God. God did not even relieve him when he spoke well of Him in the midst of all the naysayers. Job's relief came when he obeyed God's direction and prayed for his friends. What lessons can you learn from this?

PRAYER: Pray for those who have wrongfully accused you.

JUNE 27

Bill Me

Philemon 17-18 (KJV)

If thou count me therefore a partner, receive him as myself.

If he hath wronged thee, or oweth thee ought, put that on mine account

Onesimus was said to be a runaway slave who converted to Christianity when Paul met him in prison. Now a brother in Christ, Paul wrote to Philemon – one of his spiritual sons - on Onesimus' behalf. He sought to have Philemon forgive Onesimus' infractions. In fact, Paul asked Philemon to receive Onesimus not as a slave but as a brother both in Christ and in the flesh. What an impression that must have made on Onesimus! Do you ask for forgiveness on someone's behalf? Do you forgive others because Jesus forgave you?

PRAYER: Lord, I wronged You and Jesus paid the price – it was charged to His account. Please help me to forgive others because Jesus shed His blood so I have forgiveness with You. Help me to intervene on behalf of others and seek forgiveness for them.

DAY 333

JUNE 28

Romans 4: 20-21 (KJV)

> *He staggered not at the promise of God through unbelief; but was strong in faith, giving glory to God;*
>
> *And being fully persuaded that, what he had promised, he was able also to perform.*

Abraham received a promise from God – he and his wife would have a son! However, years came and went. Nothing happened. Excitement faded. Hope waned. Yet Abraham's faith remained strong. God had spoken. Even when it seemed like time was running out and the promise was not going to be fulfilled, he kept believing. He did not doubt. He was fully persuaded that God would fulfill His promise. Sometimes the promises of God may take time to manifest but remain steadfast in who God is. Everything He promised will come to pass. No matter how long it takes, He is watching over every single Word to perform it.

DECLARATION: As Abraham staggered not at the promise of God through unbelief, so too I, (**insert your name**), stagger not at the promises of God through unbelief. I am strong in faith, giving glory to God. I am fully persuaded that, what God has promised He is able to perform.

JUNE 29

Prayer for the Saints

Colossians 1:3 (KJV)

We give thanks to God and the Father of our Lord Jesus Christ, praying always for you

In Paul's epistle to the church at Colossae he mentioned that he was always praying for them, particularly he was praying prayers of thanksgiving. These persons seemed to have recently accepted Christ and were demonstrating noteworthy faith. Not only that, they also demonstrated sincere love to all of their brothers in Christ. This is a remarkable account. It is a guide to us in how to help new converts. It is our duty to pray continuously for persons who accept Jesus as their Saviour and Lord. Pray for their growth, their faith, their desire for the Word and their preservation through grace.

CHALLENGE: Make a list of persons have recently accepted Christ and pray for them.

JUNE 30

Rejected for Christ

Luke 21:16 (KJV)

And ye shall be betrayed both by parents, and brethren, and kinsfolks, and friends; and some of you shall they cause to be put to death.

Sometimes close relationships are compromised when one person accepts Jesus Christ as Saviour. When this happens there is pain, rejection and confusion. However, God provides comfort. God will always be with His children - those who accept salvation through Jesus Christ. He will never leave them. He will be with His children in the fire, in death's valley, and in trouble. Even if you are forced to confront the possibility of death for Christ's sake, remember that Jesus promised that you will win life. May you choose Christ and all that comes with that choice.

PRAYER: Pray for Christians who are hurting because others rejected them when they accepted Christ as Lord and Saviour.

DAY 336

JULY 1

He Hears

Psalm 34:15 (KJV)

> *The eyes of the LORD are upon the righteous, and his ears are open unto their cry.*

God is always watching over His children, the righteous. In fact His children are held in the palm of His hands. In living we experience pain – emotional pain, psychological pain and physical pain. We cry when we are hurt or distressed. No matter how softly we cry, God hears it because we live in Him. The Lord hears the cry of His children and when He hears our cry He responds. He provides comfort.

DECLARATION: The Lord hears my cry and comforts me.

DAY 337

JULY 2

My First Love

Revelation 2:4 (KJV)

Nevertheless I have somewhat against thee, because thou hast left thy first love.

Do you get butterflies in your stomach when you think about God? Do you anxiously await spending time with Him? Do you talk to Him? Do you want to get to know Him more? Do you do the things that will give Him pleasure? Do you tell others about Him? God expects us to maintain the initial degree of love that we had for Him. He expects that love to grow. Take a minute to do some introspection. Have you abandoned your zeal for Christ? Do you still rejoice for the gift of salvation? Do you tenderly remember that it is God's love for you that makes you "alive in Christ"? If you do not feel the same way about God as you did when you first accepted Christ as your Saviour it means that you have left your first love.

PRAYER: Father, I want to love You as I first did. You are my first love. I return to You O Lord.

DAY 338

JULY 3

1 Thessalonians 5: 12-13 (KJV)

> *And we beseech you, brethren, to know them which labour among you, and are over you in the Lord, and admonish you;*
>
> *And to esteem them very highly in love for their work's sake. And be at peace among yourselves*

God has placed spiritual leaders in our lives. These persons labour for you – they contend for you in the spiritual realm, they provide wise counsel, they intercede for you and they correct you. Such persons are to be honoured. You are to honour them because they labour for you. So, honour your Sunday/Sabbath School teacher, your evangelists, ministers, pastors and prophets. Hold them in the highest regard. Do not become familiar or get cheeky.

CHALLENGE: Choose a spiritual leader and honour him/her in a tangible way today.

DAY 339

JULY 4

Pray for the Peace of Jerusalem

Psalm 122:6 (KJV)

> *Pray for the peace of Jerusalem: they shall prosper that love thee.*

Praying for the peace of Jerusalem – the physical place or the church – should be a daily prayer. Peace is essential to the success of a nation and of any church. When you pray for the peace of Jerusalem you are also bringing peace upon yourself as the Lord promised prosperity for those who pray for Jerusalem's peace. Remember Obed-Edom? He loved the house of God and that love cause him to keep the Ark of the Covenant in his house. For doing this he experienced unprecedented blessings. Be sure to include 'let there be peace in Jerusalem' as a prayer point on your prayer list.

PRAYER: O Lord let there be peace in Jerusalem.

JULY 5

Revelation

Revelation 1:1 (KJV)

> *The Revelation of Jesus Christ, which God gave unto him, to shew unto his servants things which must shortly come to pass; and he sent and signified it by his angel unto his servant John*

The book of Revelation is a revelation of Jesus. It is also a revelation from Jesus. As awesome as that is, many Christians fear this book. However that fear is unfounded. First, remember that God did not give us the spirit of fear. Second, remember that Jesus is good and there is no need to have negative emotions to the one who volunteered to die so you can enjoy eternal life in a place that He went to prepare. Delve in the book of Revelation to see Jesus.

PRAYER: Lord, please help me to understand the book of Revelation as I read it.

JULY 6

Read and be Blessed

Revelation 1:3 (KJV)

> *Blessed is he that readeth, and they that hear the words of this*
> *prophecy, and keep those things which are written therein:*
> *for the time is at hand.*

Revelation is the only book of the Bible that God promises to bless you for reading it. Yet, the enemy has kept many Christians away by planting seeds of fear of the book. Those seeds have been replicated in millions of lives many generations later. However, today you know that there is a blessing for those who read Revelation! Take up your Bible and begin to read. Turn on your audio Bible and begin to listen to the book of Revelation. Do not short change yourself. How remarkable is it that you can activate a blessing by simply reading?

CHALLENGE: Arrange a Bible Reading Meeting with three of your friends and read through the book of Revelation.

DAY 342

JULY 7

Christian Greeting

2 John 1:3 (KJV)

> *Grace be with you, mercy, and peace, from God the Father,*
> *and from the Lord Jesus Christ, the Son of the Father, in*
> *truth and love.*

What a beautiful greeting! Here we see John the Evangelist greeting honourable Christians with the level of dignity due to them. I think that by this greeting a lot was accomplished: a prayer was prayed – 'let grace cover your sins, let peace vanquish your miseries and let peace abound in your life'; and blessings imparted. How wonderful if we would greet other Christians in the same manner today.

CHALLENGE: Greet each Christian by saying, 'Grace, mercy and peace be with you'.

JULY 8

Be Strong in Grace

2 Timothy 2:1(a) (KJV)

> *Thou therefore, my son, be strong in the grace that is in Christ Jesus.*
>
> *And the things that thou hast heard of me among many witnesses, the same commit thou to faithful men, who shall be able to teach others also.*

Timothy was Paul's son in the faith. Paul commanded him to be strong. The command was not to be physically strong but to be strong in Jesus, in the sanctification that comes from Him and through Him. Timothy was to teach faithful men the same things that Paul taught him. He was to disciple them so that they could in turn teach others. It is important that you grow in the grace and knowledge of Jesus Christ because one day you will be required to teach other believers (faithful men) so that they can teach others.

PRAYER: Lord, cause me to grow in Your grace and give me the ability to teach about You.

DAY 344

JULY 9

May They Be Proud

2 Timothy 1:5 (KJV)

When I call to remembrance the unfeigned faith that is in thee, which dwelt first in thy grandmother Lois, and thy mother Eunice; and I am persuaded that in thee also.

Paul was Timothy's mentor. Timothy ardently held to what he was taught by his parents and by Paul. Paul was proud of Timothy because he had an honest faith. He did not pretend to have faith in God. His faith in God was real and pure. Your parents have taught you. Your mentors have imparted to you. Will you be a faithful mentee/student? Will your conduct and achievement make your parents, teachers and mentors proud?

PRAYER: Father, please give me grace to do the things that will make You, my parents, my teachers and my mentors proud of me, in Jesus name. Amen

DAY 345

JULY 10

In the Right Place, at the Right Time

Luke 2:7 (KJV)

> *And she brought forth her firstborn son, and wrapped him in swaddling clothes, and laid him in a manger; because there was no room for them in the inn.*

How often do you wish that you were born to different parents in a different country? When I was growing up I did! Almost every day. I had that wish because I was born in a poor community where subsistence farming was the main economic activity. Jesus, the son of God, was born in a manger. He came in a specific place at a specific time for a specific purpose. I never appreciated that the geographical location of my birth was divinely orchestrated. But, today I can tell you that you were born to your parents in a specific community at a specific time for a specific purpose. Despite the circumstances of His birth, Jesus fulfilled His purpose. Will you?

PRAYER: Ask God to show you His purpose for your life so that you can fulfill it.

DAY 346

JULY 11

Submitted to His Will

St. Matthew 26: 39, 42, 44 (KJV)

And he went a little farther, and fell on his face, and prayed, saying, O my Father, if it be possible, let this cup pass from me: nevertheless not as I will, but as thou wilt.

He went away again the second time, and prayed, saying, O my Father, if this cup may not pass away from me, except I drink it, thy will be done.

And he left them, and went away again, and prayed the third time, saying the same words.

Sometimes when the heaviness of your task becomes a glaring reality you may ask God to take it from you but, remember that He chose you to do that thing because He has every confidence in you. He knows you will succeed. If you need to, pray as Jesus did.

PRAYER: Lord, I thank You for trusting me with this task. It sometimes become overwhelming and I want to quit however, please give me the strength to get it done so that Your will may be fulfilled. I thank You for the success of this task in Jesus name, amen.

DAY 347

JULY 12

O to Be Faithful

1 Corinthians 4:2 (KJV)

> *Moreover it is required in stewards, that a man be found faithful.*

A steward is a person employed to look after the affairs of another. Based on this definition, you are God's steward. You are looking after His affairs in the earth. How has your stewardship been? You are also an earthly steward. Your parents may have given you some aspect of the home to be responsible for. Likewise, you teacher may have given you a role to help maintain discipline in your school. How well do you do your duties? Are you loyal, devoted, committed and dedicated? These are some of the traits of a faithful person.

PRAYER: O Lord, grace to be faithful.

DAY 348

JULY 13

Psalm 90:12 (KJV)

> *So teach us to number our days, that we may apply our hearts unto wisdom.*

The person who lives to be 70 years old has 25,550 days in his life. God promised us 120 years. There are 43,800 days in 120 years! How many days have you lived so far? Have you done anything to glorify God in that time? Has anyone benefitted from your life? Will anyone benefit from your life? Each day is one less day from the number you started out with. How many days do you have left in the average lifespan? Take a step to make them be of value to someone.

CHALLENGE: Answer each question on a sheet of paper. Based on your answers, determine what actions you need to take.

DAY 349

JULY 14

Eternal Weight of Glory

2 Corinthian 4:17 (KJV)

For our light affliction, which is but for a moment, worketh for us a far more exceeding and eternal weight of glory;

Every difficulty, obstacle, trial and impediment helps to build our character. Despite how burdensome our afflictions may be, they are made light because we are supported by the arms of Almighty God. Enduring these afflictions are a way for us to sever out hearts from the world and focus our hearts and eyes on Christ. Their effect is to help us to achieve the eternal glory that God had provided.

PRAYER: Father please help me remember that the things I go through are momentary and they are working so that I will have the eternal glory that You have prepared for me, in Jesus name. Amen.

DAY 350

JULY 15

In His Name

St. John 14:14 (KJV)

If ye shall ask any thing in my name, I will do it.

Jesus promised that **whatever** we ask in His name He will do it so that God may be glorified. This simply means that you will have whatsoever you ask for in Jesus' name, according to God's will. Do you know the will of God concerning your life? It is in the Bible. Daily remind yourself of His will and ask Jesus to fulfill His will in your life. You'll be pleasantly surprised at what you see!

CONFESSION: I have authority to use Jesus' name. Whatsoever I ask in the name of Jesus, according to God's will, He will do.

JULY 16

Required Love

St. Matthew 22:37 (KJV)

> *Jesus said unto him, Thou shalt love the Lord thy God with
> all thy heart, and with all thy soul, and with all thy mind.*

What does it mean to love God in this way? To me, it means we should submit to Him totally. It means being sincere, not just saying that we love Him but demonstrating love by obeying His Words. You have to love Him with everything that you are, with your very life! The command to love God is the greatest commandment. None of us have the capacity to fulfill this commandment on our own. Loving God in the manner required can only be fulfilled by the grace of our Lord Jesus Christ and by the help of the Holy Spirit. Ask Him to help you.

PRAYER: Pray that your entire being will actively love God.

DAY 352

JULY 17

His Choosing

1 Corinthians 1:27 (KJV)

> *But God hath chosen the foolish things of the world to confound the wise; and God hath chosen the weak things of the world to confound the things which are mighty*

God uses plain ordinary people to do extraordinary things for Him. That is just the way He is. If you examine the scriptures you will notice that those who thought themselves wise were not used by God. Yet, unlearned men – poor fishermen of lowly parentage – were used by God to do the unimaginable. They were chosen and entrusted with the responsibility of being the carriers of the gospel of grace and peace. This may seem foolish as there were many learned Jews in that time however, in these weak vessels God's power and splendor was placed on full display for all to see.

PRAYER: Lord, I make myself available to be used by You.

DAY 353

JULY 18

Colossians 3:16 (KJV)

> *Let the word of Christ dwell in you richly in all wisdom;*
> *teaching and admonishing one another in psalms and hymns*
> *and spiritual songs, singing with grace in your hearts to the*
> *Lord.*

Let your heart be the dwelling place of the Word. Let the Word abide in your heart. When this happens you will become wise as the wisdom that the Word dwells in is the wisdom of Christ. Use the psalms, hymns and spiritual songs as teaching tools. Use them to teach others of the gospel of grace. Let the psalms, hymns and spiritual songs minister to you. Today you are invited to read and think on God's Word until it fills your heart and mind.

DECLARATION: The Word of God dwells in me richly.

DAY 354

JULY 19

1 Corinthians 11:31 (KJV)

For if we would judge ourselves, we should not be judged.

Self-examination. Introspection. It is important that we look into ourselves for the things that are not Christ-like and then seek to correct them. This search must be an honest examination. If we do this we will not experience the chastening of God because we would have, on our own, corrected wrongdoings. It is important for you to examine yourself and straighten out your life with God's help. Do not allow things to get to the point where God has to initiate the straightening.

CHALLENGE: Begin self-examination today.

DAY 355

JULY 20

Be Willing and Obedient

Isaiah 1:19 (KJV)

If you are willing and obedient, you shall eat the good of the land.

God wants you to have the best temporal blessings imaginable. He wants you to get good grades in school, and to have the best things in life. It is very important that you work together with Him so that you can have those things. If you willingly submit to His rules and obey His directives you and all that you plant will be protected by God – your crops, your ideas, your investments. They will yield much increase and not be affected by worms – the external factors that cause decline.

CONFESSION: I will walk according to God's Word. I will love Him. I will serve Him. I am willing and obedient therefore, I will eat the good of the land.

JULY 21

Hang On!

Hebrews 10:23 (KJV)

> *Let us hold fast the profession of our faith without wavering;*
> *(for he is faithful that promised;)*

Hold tenaciously to the promise of eternal life. Do not doubt or wonder whether the promises of God are true. They are. You can always hang on to God's promises because what He says will occur. God has never been proven to be untrustworthy since the world began and He will never be.

DECLARATION: I hold firmly to my confession of faith in God without wavering.

DAY 357

JULY 22

His Grace is Sufficient

2 Corinthians 12:9 (KJV)

> *And he said unto me, My grace is sufficient for thee: for my strength is made perfect in weakness. Most gladly therefore will I rather glory in my infirmities, that the power of Christ may rest upon me.*

No matter how great the trial, how deep the need or how acute the weakness, God's grace is enough to keep you sane and to make you endure. His grace will always prove to be of greater value to you than even the answer to a prayer to remove the weakness that you are facing. It is in our weakness that we appreciate God's strength. It is in our weakness that we truly begin to understand that strength. Therefore, Paul saw it as a privilege to be afflicted because that situation brought him into direct contact with God's strength, a strength which reinvigorated him. God's grace can be the same for you. His grace can do the same for you.

DECLARATION: God's grace is sufficient for me.

DAY 358

JULY 23

Psalm 3:5 (KJV)

I laid me down and slept; I awaked; for the LORD sustained me.

Sleep is said to be the closest that humans come to death. During sleep we are unaware of what is happening. We have no control over our faculties. When David wrote this Psalm he was a wanderer having been exiled from his home. However, despite the danger he was able to enjoy restful sleep and awake unharmed. David realized that this was not of his doing. You cannot wake from sleep on your own; God keeps you during sleep and He caused you to wake to another day. This is something to be thankful for. It is something for which you should glorify Him.

PRAYER: Thank God for keeping you while you slept last night and for waking you up this morning.

DAY 359

JULY 24

Do it Willingly

Philippians 2:14 (KJV)

Do all things without murmurings and disputings.

Whatever you do, do it obediently, willingly and cheerfully. So often we do not want to do something and we sulk all the way through. Sometimes we even make the experience uncomfortable for others. When undertaking a task, do it cheerfully. Do not get into disputes or murmurings with others about what should be done and who should do it. A cheerful countenance will alleviate the burden of all your tasks.

DECLARATION: I do all things obediently, willingly and cheerfully to bring God glory.

DAY 360

JULY 25

Psalm 147:4 (KJV)

> *He telleth the number of the stars; he calleth them all by their names.*

How many stars are there in the universe? Did you begin to think about the question? The stars are innumerable. It is a fact that no astronomer has been able to quantify the number of stars in existence but God know each one by its name! How incredible! The stars are named and each is known by God. The inherent power of God that this represents is unfathomable! What intellectual capacity could enable one to do that? It is this amazing Sovereign that you serve. It is this incredible God that has covenanted with you. Imagine that?!

PRAYER: Lord, I thank You that Your intelligence is above and beyond human comprehension.

JULY 26

Alpha and Omega

Revelation 1:8 (KJV)

> *I am Alpha and Omega, the beginning and the ending, saith the Lord, which is, and which was, and which is to come, the Almighty.*

Jesus is revealed as the beginning and the ending. He is the beginning and ending of all things. He was at the beginning and He will be at the end. Jesus has always exist and He will always exist. He is the Almighty. No matter what happens in life, always remember that Jesus is the beginning and ending of all things therefore you are secure in Him.

DECLARATION: Jesus is the Alpha and Omega, the beginning and the ending. I am in Him. I am secure in Him.

DAY 362

JULY 27

Children of God

Romans 8:16-17 (AMP)

> *The Spirit Himself [thus] testifies together with our own spirit, [assuring us] that we are children of God.*
>
> *And if we are [His] children, then we are [His] heirs also: heirs of God and fellow heirs with Christ [sharing His inheritance with Him]; only we must share His suffering if we are to share His glory*

Jesus is the first born of many children. You are God's child. You were adopted into the family! It means that God is your father and Jesus is your brother. Whatever God has disposed of in His will is to be given to all his children therefore, you are a joint-heir with Jesus. That means you share inheritance with Him. You will share God's legacy with Him. The only catch is that you must share in His suffering. That is in large measure denying yourself the sinful pleasures of the world and bearing the rejection of the world in the same spirit that He did.

CONFESSION: God is my father therefore I am a joint-heir with Jesus.

JULY 28

My Duty

Ecclesiastes 12:13 (KJV)

> *Let us hear the conclusion of the whole matter: Fear God, and keep his commandments: for this is the whole duty of man.*

In conclusion of all that has been said and written by wise men, we can conclude that our entire duty to God is to fear Him and do the things He tells us to do. Trust Him. Reverence Him. Obey Him. That is your entire business and in it you will find abundant joy and peace.

CHALLENGE: Decide to start doing your duty. If you have already started, decide to continue doing your duty.

DAY 364

JULY 29

The Power of Words

Hebrews 11:3 (KJV)

> *Through faith we understand that the worlds were framed by the word of God, so that things which are seen were not made of things which do appear.*

God created the world by speaking words. You were made in God's image. Your words are creative. They create situations in your life. They create your future. If you say you will fail then you will indeed fail. If you say you will succeed be sure to start planning the celebration party because you will succeed. Since words have such immense power, you should only say what aligns with what God said. Watch over your words. Ensure that you do not speak negative things in jest. Speak positive things and watch them come to past. Frame your life.

DECLARATION: Whatever I say will be in keeping with what God has said. I will speak my world into being.

DAY 365

JULY 30

1 Timothy 1:17 (KJV)

> *Now unto the King eternal, immortal, invisible, the only wise*
> *God, be honour and glory for ever and ever. Amen.*

Paul was overcome with gratitude for saving grace. This was so much so that he seemed to have interrupted his train of thought to give God glory! God is worthy of honour. He is the eternal King. He is immortal! He is God of the Ages. All honour and glory to God forever! Let us respect and praise Him forever and evermore.

DECLARATION: All glory and praise be to the Immortal King – God of the Ages. Honour and glory be Yours for ever and ever.

DAY 366

July 31

I Will Continue in Prayer

O Lord, like Hannah I will continue praying before You – **1 Samuel 1:12**

I will give myself continually to prayer and to the ministry of the Word – **Acts 6:4**

I will rejoice in hope, be patient in tribulation, and continue steadfastly in prayer – **Romans 12:12**

I will continue in the temple praising and blessing God – **St. Luke 24:53**

I will hope continually and will praise You yet more and more O God – **Psalm 71:14**

God, like Daniel, I will continue in prayer and service – **Daniel 1:21**

I will take heed to myself and to the doctrine. I will continue in them so that I may be saved – **1 Timothy 4:16**

I will continue in all things that I have learned and been assured of, knowing from whom I have learned them – **2 Timothy 3:14**

I will continue steadfast in the apostle's doctrine and fellowship, in the breaking of bread and in prayers – **Acts 2:42**

With purpose of heart I will continue with God – **Acts 11:23**

O God let the truth of the gospel continue with me – **Galatians 2:5**

Father, I ask for grace to bless You at all times; Your praise shall continually be in my mouth – **Psalm 34:1**

Lord, I will continually offer the sacrifice of praise to You and the fruit of my lips, giving praise to Your name – **Hebrews 13:15**

CPSIA information can be obtained
at www.ICGtesting.com
Printed in the USA
BVHW041108161219
566814BV00012B/184/P